Trinity's Conscious Kitchen

Inspiring soul through conscious cuisine

~ Trinity Bourne ~

Openhand Press

Book design by Trinity Bourne.

Photography by Trinity Bourne
except images on pages 4, 5, 11, 25, 37, 58, 63,
65, 71, 93, 96, 117, 120, 122, 124, 127, 128, 136,
148, 153(bottom), 157 & 159
which are from www.colourbox.com
and image on page 7 which is from the
5Gateways documentary film
www.5Gateways.com

ISBN 978-0-9556792-1-6

Visit: www.trinityskitchen.com

I dedicate this book to my mum, Susan, for giving me the incredible gift of life. The patience, unconditional love and commitment you have shown me over the years have touched me deeply. Your resourcefulness and ability to create delicious cuisine out of whatever is available has been a much appreciated source of soul food on my own journey. You are a wonderful 'teacher', in the true sense of the word, leading by example.

I'd like to extend a special and heartfelt thanks to everyone who has encouraged me to write this book over the past decade. It has been an incredible exploration that would never have happened without so many enthusiastic people who've shared my food saying "you've got to write a book!" There are so many of you! A loving thanks to my chief recipe testing team Ocean, Mark, Fiona, Becky, Bethan and David. Boundless thanks and appreciation to Open, Pennie, Fiona and Ben for your invaluable efforts in proof reading. It has been awesome to share this epic adventure with you all.

I offer my deepest soul inspired thanks to Open, my beloved husband and chief recipe taster. I feel eternally grateful for your presence and loving support. You've been in it with me all the way. I love you beyond measure!

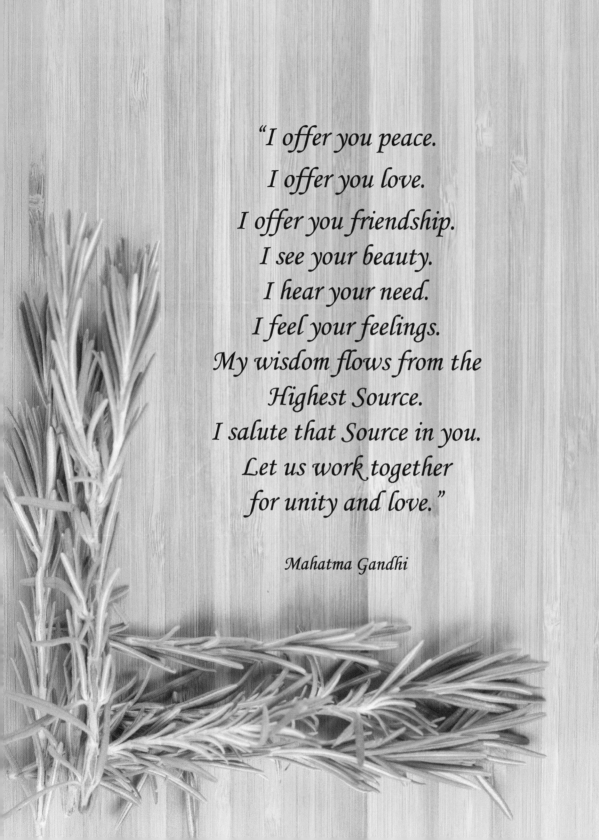

"I offer you peace.
I offer you love.
I offer you friendship.
I see your beauty.
I hear your need.
I feel your feelings.
My wisdom flows from the
Highest Source.
I salute that Source in you.
Let us work together
for unity and love."

Mahatma Gandhi

CONTENTS

Welcome...

Trinity's Conscious Kitchen is a divinely inspired invitation into a world of transformational conscious eating. It is an open gateway to a higher vibrational paradigm.

Everything is energy! The energy of our food directly impacts sentient life on all levels. By embracing a plant based diet of the most conscious kind (organic, local, home grown) we find a natural affinity and respect for all life. We begin to steadily raise our vibration and attune to the divine flow of the universe.

Most people who eat this way not only experience optimal health, but also greater spiritual, mental and emotional clarity. As well as nurturing our own body on a physical level, we honour Mother Earth, facilitating an infusion of energy to catalyse our spiritual growth.

All of the recipes here have been prepared and created lovingly to share an energy designed to infuse ever greater levels of higher consciousness into our world. They invite you to explore what is right for you; to enfold what resonates into your daily life and allow your radiant beingness to permeate ever further outwards touching those around you.

This book has been inspired by listening to the guidance of my soul. I encourage us all to listen to the soul and embrace the unique guidance it brings as we journey into a higher paradigm of conscious food preparation and spiritual evolution.

Soul to Soul
Trinity

THE DAY THAT CHANGED MY LIFE FOREVER

"At some point in our journey of life, the soul wakes up."

I don't quite know why it happened to me when it did. I could call it destiny or even fate, but honestly, I think it was simply because my time had come. I was ready.

"Who am I?"

"Where do I belong?"

"Why am I here?"

"What is my purpose?"

"What is the point to it all?"

I just couldn't help it. My soul was tormented by the relentless yearning to find meaning in a meaningless world. I'd never been content with the 9 to 5 treadmill. I sensed that there was more to life - so much more; an uncharted realm of soul that I'd yet to embrace. Submerged in a world where I just didn't fit, I felt an intolerable pain; a primal scream from the depths of my being. By the end of my teenage years, I became increasingly depressed as I struggled to unleash the purpose of life. It was as if I was buried and hidden at the core of my being. At that point, I wanted to give my life back and dissolve into the void from which I'd once emerged. I wanted to die. I'd reached the bottom of the well of grief. It was barren, dry and empty. My world caved in. I collapsed.

Ready and willing to surrender my life to the universe; to hand it back; give up the fight and throw the towel in, I did! I gave it back. Everything I'd ever loved, dreamed of, hoped for, everything I wanted, everything I didn't want. Without exception, I gave it all back. *"Here universe - take it - I give up - take it all back, take me back, I don't belong here - I've searched the depths of the universe and I can't find what I am looking for - take me back'*. In that moment, without even knowing it, I had surrendered, every cell of my being to the divine.

Then, it happened...

As I lay there, collapsed, unable to feel anything anymore, something totally extraordinary took place. A white light began to surge from the core of my being. It was like the white water of a thousand mighty waterfalls, flooding every cell within me. The light dissolved everything it touched, consuming me entirely, radiating the entire field around, until there was nothing, but white light. The whole universe disappeared. There was no me or you; no this or that; no up or down. The veil had fallen away and all that was left was one pulsating white light of pure unity consciousness. It formed everything, lacked nothing, whilst exuding a paradoxical formlessness. I was that, that was me and so was everything else. All there was, was white light. There were no boundaries, no beginning, no end. It was the 'oneness' that gurus and sages have talked about for aeons, except at the time, I'd never heard anyone speak about it. It was a pure experience, without any frame of intellectual reference or influence from the mind to taint it.

I experienced the soul of all other sentient beings, trees, creatures, people, all forms of life all at once, all connected as one pulsating energy. Judgment of 'good' or 'bad' fell away. I transcended into a higher realm of unity and oneness. This was what my soul had been searching for all these years. The experience imparted the wordless 'secrets' of the universe to me. They were given, to integrate and embody as an aspect of my beingness - beyond the intellect - so that in turn, I could share soul to soul, by reflection and deep inner knowing with those who I would come to meet in the years that followed. For a long time, I couldn't even put it into words, but instead found ways to share the energy as it infused into the things I did.

"There was no me or you; no this or that; no up or down. The veil had fallen away and all that was left was one pulsating white light of pure unity consciousness."

After an experience like that everything changes. Life can never be the same again. Everything was different. There were no boundaries. I experienced the interconnectedness of all things. Not as a concept, but as a living, breathing experiential way of life. I witnessed the light at the heart of all life and saw that we are all united. What we do to another, we inevitably do to ourselves. We are inseparable by nature.

Having let go of everything, I arrived. I found myself. The light of my soul was unleashed and fully awakened. I'd come 'home'.

At that time, I had no idea that the experience would be the source of divine inspiration that would guide me for the rest of my life. And, of course, from that moment onwards, everything changed.

A CONSCIOUS KITCHEN IS BORN

There are many things that affect our vibration, although what we eat is one of the most obvious. What I ate changed instantly in that experience of divine awakening. Without a second to lose, I turned instantaneously to a compassionate diet, omitting meat, dairy and all other animal products from my food choices. In the twenty years since, I have never once looked back or felt any less of an impulse to eat in this way. Feeling the interconnectedness of all life, I can't knowingly cause harm to my fellow sentient beings.

I began to care about what I ate, where it came from and how it had been produced. I began to make conscious choices. The energy of my physical body began to align with the loving pulse of the universe almost straight away. Eating consciously began to raise my vibration to one much more aligned with higher consciousness. The light of my soul began to flood into my life more and more. My spiritual evolution began to skyrocket.

Over the years, I felt moved to share the extraordinary gift that I'd been given by the universe - to share, so that others could awaken it within themselves. One such way was through consciousness raising cuisine. Earlier in my journey I opened my home to host regular raw food vegan pot-luck buffets. I'd engage with the most fascinating health seekers, delighting for hours in conversations about conscious food creation. As that chapter in my life came to a close, I met my soul mate, who I soon after married. In 2006, after many years of exploration and fun, I introduced conscious catering to the residential spiritual retreats and workshops that we facilitate together. I wanted to find a way to show people that eating consciously can be both delicious and inspiring. Conscious food creation has been helping to inspire the evolution of many bright and shining souls ever since. I really have to thank the myriad of beautiful people in my life who've come and gone over the years, enjoying my creations, ceaselessly encouraging me to write this book.

A CONSCIOUS BRIDGE

Trinity's Conscious Kitchen is designed as a bridge between the old and the new. I've created this book both for people new to conscious eating and those who've been embracing it for some time already. You'll find something for everyone - from delicious comforting 'grounding' main meals and desserts, to lighter, pranic-packed salads and dips. There are plenty of new and original vibrational raising recipes for all skill levels; created over the years in my own conscious kitchen.

"Feeling the interconnectedness of all life, I can't knowingly cause harm to my fellow sentient beings."

WE DON'T LIVE IN A PERFECT WORLD

The natural ecosystems in our world have been radically tampered with. Foods have been hybridised and genetically modified, causing harm that we can only begin to imagine. Even with the healthiest diet and best will in the world, we are bombarded by pollutants, pesticides, harmful chemicals, radiation and electro-smog.

So, we need to do our part to re-balance things. We all need a Conscious Kitchen to give ourselves and our families the opportunity to experience optimal health in an unbalanced world. Always choose organic, pesticide free, chemical free, home grown or locally produced foods wherever possible. Embrace nature's superfoods (which are even available for many of us by foraging and growing our own). Welcome sunshine, pure water, meditation, conscious exercise and conscious living to raise your vibration and optimise beingness.

BEING VEGAN IN A NUTSHELL

As you'll remember from my original story, when I woke up, I moved pretty much instantly to a vegan way of life. The divine guidance of my soul showed me that all life is sacred and consuming a compassionate diet was optimal not only for myself, but all beings. I started to see that if I was healthy and vibrant, then I could better serve my purpose in life - whatever that would be.

Back then, twenty years ago, being vegan was much less common than it is today. Now there is a plethora of insight and support out there to help along the way. More and more people have realised the amazing benefits that can be had from eating a plant based diet. It is much easier to find vegan, organic, local food out and about these days.

ALL LIFE IS SACRED

Back in the 1990s, as I explored deeper, I came to learn the sad truth about the dairy and animal industry. I'd see photos and read reports of how chickens were treated like batteries, with an appalling quality of life. I learned how other animals were used like inanimate objects, forced to produce food for willing consumers. I found out that in order for a cow to produce milk, she'd usually be kept in degrading conditions, like a machine, having her calf taken away from her almost instantly at birth. As if that were not enough, she'd be forced to produce considerably more milk than she ever naturally would, putting a crippling strain upon her system - on a daily basis.

'Happy cows' living in fields or 'happy chickens' with more freedom - are really just 'happier slaves' who have a few more freedoms, until their time is up. The truth is, slaughter is slaughter. One day whilst camping in the countryside, I listened to one mother cow, literally 'screaming' out for hours, distraught with terror after her calf had been taken from her, so that she could be milked for human beings instead.

I've seen the living, feeling sentience in these amazing creatures time and time again. On another occasion whilst out for a walk in the Glastonbury countryside, I observed several cows in great distress after witnessing one of their fellow cows keel over and die in the field. It was abundantly clear that they felt emotional pain, just like people do when a loved one passes away.

All life is sacred. Life is a gift. As human beings, we really don't have the right to desecrate other sentient life.

After digging further still, I soon discovered how destructive meat and dairy production was on the environment too. The Vegan Society, gives an excellent overview of how this is so:

"A University of Chicago study found that the 'typical' US diet generates the equivalent of nearly 1.5 tonnes more carbon dioxide per person per year than a vegan diet. The livestock industry is responsible for 18% of global greenhouse gas emissions, more than the entire transport sector (which produces 13.5%), including aviation.

Plant-based diets only require around one third of the land and water needed to produce a typical Western diet. Farmed animals consume much more protein, water and calories than they produce, so far greater quantities of crops and water are needed to produce animal 'products' to feed humans than are needed to feed people direct on a plant-based diet. With water and land becoming scarcer globally, world hunger increasing and the planet's population rising, it is much more sustainable to eat plant foods direct than use up precious resources feeding farmed animals.

Farming animals and growing their feed also contributes to other environmental problems such as deforestation, water pollution and land degradation." (Vegan Society)

In 2006 the Food and Agriculture Organisation showed that 'the global livestock industry' is in the top three causes of all major environmental problems, including climate change. For facts and further information on this you can find an extensive PDF document called 'Livestock's Long Shadow': environmental issues and opinions, here: http://www.fao.org/docrep/010/a0701e/a0701e00.HTM

Optimal health

Many people feel, based on personal experience, that the human body is designed to live on plant foods. Soon after starting to eat purely vegan food, I began to feel much happier and healthier. A diet without meat and other animal products frees up a lot of energy, so that the body can get on with other important functions, such as repair, cleansing and rejuvenation. I know people who have totally regained a vibrant, youthful health during life threatening illnesses or crippling arthritis by eating consciously and going dairy-free or vegan.

It's also important to remember that everything carries energy. Animals who have been slaughtered and especially those who've been treated like machines, carry a lot of fear and negative energy (understandably so). If we consume them, we take that energy into our own system too, which inevitably effects our vibration, health and energy levels.

What really is natural?

Human beings are the only species in the world to knowingly drink the milk of another species. We are also the only animal on the planet to consume dairy after the age of weaning. Most people never even give this a thought. Yet if we observe nature closely, it becomes abundantly clear how denatured we humans have become.

Humans willingly consume things that are not meant for us (until we make a conscious choice not to of course). Take a natural carnivore, like a cat. She hungers for flesh. She was designed by nature with sharp claws and razor sharp teeth for ripping raw flesh apart. She was given the natural instinct to stalk, run with incredible speed and pounce. Not only that, she has a digestive system that thrives on raw flesh. When looking for answers, nature always speaks loudest. Humans do not have flesh ripping, carnivorous traits by default. That says it all!

Personally, I feel that we were never supposed to consume flesh or indeed the milk of another species.

"Everything is connected.
The choices we make in one area of life,
permeate into all other areas of our life."

SPIRITUAL EVOLUTION

Without choosing food consciously, I doubt that I would have experienced such accelerated spiritual growth. Everything is connected. The choices we make in one area of life, permeate into all other areas. True spirituality is about joining all the dots, on all levels! Compassion, love and respect for all life are tenets of higher consciousness. Conscientious food choices naturally raise our vibration, inviting powerful levels of spiritual growth.

Trinity's Conscious Kitchen naturally offers 100% purely plant based, animal free, vegan recipes. Over the years, people from all walks of life have enjoyed many of the recipes in this book before it came anywhere close to print. Even those on the most convention-al of diets have been surprised at how delicious and satisfying good vegan food can be.

CONSCIOUS FOOD CHOICES

SWEETNESS! Refined sugar is one of the most undermining, harmful food stuffs in our world today. If you look a little closer at processed food, you'll find that sugar is found in just about all of it! It has earned itself a terrible reputation for a good reason, contributing in some way, to virtually every illness in the modern era. So, it goes without saying, you won't find refined sugar in this book. You will find instead; fruits, dried fruits and other alternatives, such as apple juice concentrate and brown rice syrup. Whole fruits contain sugar that is much more suited to a healthy vibration, so I recommend them along with a few much less refined sweet alternatives. Healthy sweet alternatives can really jazz up your cuisine - although they are still best used in moderation.

WHEAT AND GLUTEN FREE-ISH

Gluten is not exactly the most vibrational raising substance! It actually acts like 'glue' ('GLU'-ten) and to put it bluntly, can wreak havoc with health. It is found in most grains to varying degrees - the worst culprit being wheat (which has been radically hybridised for the high yielding commercial market). Some people are incredibly gluten intolerant, whilst others find less hybridised grains, such as spelt, kamut, rye and barley much easier to digest than wheat. On the other hand, some people are built somewhat like tanks and appear to be able to eat whatever they like without apparent negative effect. Be aware though; food can act like a kind of anaesthetic, making us insensitive to the destructive effects that might be happening beneath the skin. So being sensitive and intolerant can conversely be a real blessing, as you have little choice but to be more conscious about what you eat. How awesome to be able make a conscious choice and take our health into our own hands as soon as we become aware that what we eat can really make a profound difference in our lives. As we cleanse and purify our system, we usually find that our body guides us away from foods that aren't in our best interest.

Personally, I don't use grains often. However, I don't feel like eliminating them entirely from the Conscious Kitchen, because grains such as spelt and barley can be awesome transitioning foods in a world where - let's face it - we sometimes need a little bit of feel good comfort. You won't find wheat used in this book at all, although we use spelt (the friendly, ancient unhybridsed cousin of wheat), barley and oats.

There are some excellent gluten free alternatives available, such as millet, quinoa, aramanth, buckwheat and rice. Embrace them and find what works for you.

A WORD ON WATER

Water is essential for health although, **'which'** water and where we get it from is a big subject of debate!

I avoid naked tap water at all costs, because it is often chlorinated and fluoridated, usually containing contaminants such as heavy metals, hormones and pesticides. I've used tap water that has been put through a reverse osmosis filter, which can taste and feel good. I prefer to leave it for a while in the sun to recharge with life force in a glass bottle or pottery urn before drinking. If you have access to water from a good reverse osmosis filter, then I'd recommend it.

Ideally we'd all have a lovely little mountain spring over the field to which we could skip, gathering it afresh every day. If you are able to get fresh spring water in your local area, then it is probably your best option (unless the land around you is used for intensive, non-organic farming or other spurious practices). We are blessed to have several springs within a reasonable distance of our home - each with very different energies. We definitely have our favourites and others that we avoid. It's all a matter of preference. Honour what you feel. Water really does carry energy - and as we absorb it, we can easily take on that vibration.

I also purchase bottled water to drink. I favour water from springs found on organic lands. Bottled water does however have a downside, with unpleasant environmental impacts. This is largely due to the incessant production of plastic or glass bottles and transportation considerations. At times however, there isn't much choice.

Investigate, explore further and always choose the most conscious choice available to you at the time.

EAT ORGANIC

As a keen gardener and supporter of my local organic markets, I can say without a doubt that organic fresh food is brimming with a vibrational-raising life force not to be tampered with. Pesticides and chemical control is an unsustainable, disrespectful solution that has long since been queuing up for disaster. It consistently fails Mother Nature, the environment, wildlife, plant life and the people it was originally designed for. Not only do toxins build up in our bodies, they have gathered in the environment exponentially, throwing local ecosystems into absolute disarray.

Whether we grow our own or buy from our local organic store, eating organic food offers a way to honour the cycle of life whilst obtaining optimal nutrition.

Raw, loving, living foods

I went through a period of my life many years ago, where I ate a purely raw, vegan diet. My energy levels shot through the roof. My spiritual journey took an evolutionary leap into the far reaches of the cosmos. I was bouncing off the walls with aliveness. I required hardly any sleep. I was shining like the sun itself. To be honest, life was absolutely amazing as a 100% raw food vegan. The food I ate was high in pranic energy, as close to it's natural state as possible. It was a necessary and invaluable experience that I wouldn't change for the world. It gave me invaluable insight into high vibrational living. I was (rather fortunately) spending quite a bit of time in Hawaii during that period, particularly in the colder months, which helped. Living in a temperate English climate on a strictly raw food diet, relying on lots of imported fresh foods, eventually became somewhat conflicting. In time, I settled somewhere in between and found that living on a 'high' raw, plant based diet worked rather well too. It basically means that I eat a lot of raw foods, although I enjoy (especially in the winter) a few cooked things too. Throughout the spectrum of all four seasons, I swing somewhere between eating 55% and 99% raw. I encourage everyone to incorporate living foods into the diet, for an extra infusion of life force - even if it's just a salad and some fresh fruit every day. It's essential for higher vibrational living. Find a happy balance that works for you.

Avoid GMOs at all costs

GMOs (genetically modified organisms) are the real 'Frankenstein' of the food world. Basically, a gene from one species is inserted to another. This process is completely unnatural and can only be achieved by highly technical means in a laboratory.

Apart from the common sense factor of 'not messing with nature', there is a growing body of evidence showing how GMOs are radically denaturing ecosystems, harming wildlife and causing damage to our bodies. One of the many issues with GMOs is the 'terminator gene', which means that plants can't reproduce naturally (in other words, you are completely beholden to the company that creates the seeds if you want to grow that crop). In nature plants normally go to seed at the end of their life, producing seeds to ensure the continued propagation of their species. For gardeners and farmers, it basically means having seeds to plant next season's crops. For Mother Earth, this means balanced and harmonious ecology. If you grow GMO or your plants cross breed with them, then you run the risk of never being able to produce your own seeds again. I urge you to look at the latest information on this subject and avoid GMOs at all costs!

NOTES FOR INTERNATIONAL READERS

MEASUREMENTS

I've used all sorts of things to determine quantities over the years. The most challenging thing about writing a recipe book has always been quantifying the ingredients. Soulful spontaneity usually means adding 'a little bit of this' and 'a little bit of that' with no thought process at all. Somehow, with a few miracles along the way, I succeeded in measuring everything. But different countries use different measurements! So, for this book, I decided in true European style (since that's where I live) to use metric measurements. If you prefer to use 'cups' or ounces instead, you'll find some handy conversion charts in the back of the book.

A lot of the recipes are quite forgiving if you add a little more or less of things. The most important thing is to relax and enjoy the experience.

DIFFERENT NAMES FOR STUFF

English is a common language, so we all tend to understand each other, although there are a few words that can cause confusion in the kitchen. Here is a handy kitchen dictionary with a few of the British and American English differences.

British English		American English
beetroot	–	beets
bicarbonate of soda	–	baking soda
cornflour	–	corn starch
courgette	–	zucchini
coriander leaf	–	cilantro
coriander seed	–	coriander
grill	–	broil
swede	–	rutabaga
sultana	–	white raisin

BEFORE YOU START

Conscious food preparation is all about the energy. When deciding what food to use I use this check list opposite...

It may not be possible to tick all of the boxes, but do have them at the forefront of your awareness. Make the most conscious choices you can and always connect consciously with your food, offering thanks.

CREATE THE SPACE

The outer space is a reflection of the inner and vice versa. All I see is part of me. So create a clean, clear space in your kitchen. Play uplifting music or sing; open the windows and listen to the birds; surround yourself with fresh window herbs; use beautiful bowls, wooden spoons and things. Enjoy the experience.

✓ BUY LOCAL

✓ BUY ORGANIC

✓ GROW YOUR OWN

✓ SUPPORT FAIR TRADE

✓ COMPOST YOUR SCRAPS

Your consciousness will permeate through the food you create – so let go of tension and stress before you begin. Create an environment that feels good. As you prepare your food, pause and take a moment to smell the fragrance of the herbs or fruits that you'll be co-creating with. Flood your senses with divine inspiration. Turn conscious food creation into a moving meditation and express it from the depths of your soul.

Enjoy, create and let your soul shine forth!

This is more than a recipe book
it's a sharing from my soul to yours.
This book is designed as an invitation
to explore deeper and find
ever higher levels of energetic vibration.
I encourage you to delve ever further into
the world of conscious living;
to embrace your connection with
Mother Earth, the cosmos
and the choices you make in every moment...

Breakfast

Breakfast is a really personal thing that can make a big difference to how we start the day. Some feel enlivened by missing it out altogether. Go with what feels right for you. For years, I've felt that eating fruit for breakfast is optimal for health and vibrancy. It gently breaks you back in from a night of fasting. Fruit requires minimal energy to digest (the digestion process can take a lot of our energy up!), freeing up your energy to heal, build and cleanse instead. Most people do however, get a bit hungry on fruit alone, and end up picking at food all morning long if they aren't satiated, in which case I'd recommend fruit along with something heavier to slow down the release of the fruit sugars.

FRUIT & TAHINI BREAKFAST MEDLEY

This is a satisfying way to eat fruit, if you need a little extra something to fill you up. Adding fat (in this case - tahini) will slow down the release of the fruit sugar in your system, giving a more sustained release of energy over the morning.

Ingredients:

Tahini
Rice milk
Raisins (optional)
Desiccated coconut (optional)
Fresh fruit non-citrus
i.e. banana, apple, pear,
   berries, mango etc.

1. Start with a heaped dessertspoon of tahini in your bowl.

2. Add a little rice milk at a time, stirring quickly and persistently to give a creamy 'mixable' texture. After adding about 2 parts liquid to 1 part tahini, you should have a lovely creamy consistency. Each batch or brand of tahini is different, so go with the flow.

3. Slice and chop as much fresh fruit as you want to eat for breakfast. For me that might consist of any combination of banana, apple, mango, pear or berries. I often just use apple. *Note: Melon is best eaten alone and on an empty stomach as it digests faster than other fruits (which can cause digestive upset when mixed with other foods) - so avoid mixing melon with this medley.*

4. Mix the fresh fruit into the tahini sauce, along with a small handful of raisins. If the sauce thickens too much, making it difficult to mix, then add a dash of water or rice milk to loosen it up again (but take care not to add too much liquid, otherwise you'll lose the creaminess - which is the whole point).

5. Sprinkle a little desiccated coconut on top and enjoy your tasty breakfast!

How To Make A Smoothie

The wonderful thing about smoothie making is being creative with what you have available. So, rather than listing a section of different recipes, I thought I'd share suggestions and tips to inspire your own creativity.

The key ingredient in a smoothie is usually banana. People enjoy the sweetness and creamy texture, although any creamy fruit will work. Every place in the world has it's own little gems. When I stay in Hawaii with my mother, she'll bring home all kinds of amazing fruits. Cherimoya, sapote, mango, papaya all make an excellent base for smoothies. Embrace whatever you have around you. Here in Glastonbury, my favourite season is the summer with local wild berries and garden berries galore.

Tip One *'how to make it super creamy'*
One of the secrets to making a really creamy 'soft ice cream like' smoothie is to freeze the banana first (a great use for any rapidly ripening bananas sitting in the fruit bowl).

Tip Two *'how to freeze a banana'*
Freeze the banana by removing the skin and then chopping into slices. Pop into a container (or freezer bag) and freeze immediately. It will be ready the next day if required (or will still be fine the next month if you forget about it).

Tip Three *'ripe, ripe, ripe'*
Use only ripe fruit. Eating unripe fruit is a big no no in the conscious kitchen! Ripe is the way nature intended fruit to be eaten and it digests much more easily.

Tip Four *'be a great explorer'*
The best ever smoothies always seem to happen by 'accident'. Of course, there's no such thing as an accident. When you really let go and have fun, the soul is unleashed - magical things happen. So don't be afraid to try new things and experiment.

Which Blender?
I like using a hand blender for just about everything. It's really easy to clean and cuts right down on the washing up. Any decent jug blender will do as well, although, if you are really into blending then you might like to invest in a powerful blender like a Vitamix.

Smoothie basics

Basic smoothie ingredients:
1 frozen banana
1 fresh ripe banana (unfrozen)
1 cup vanilla rice milk/
coconut milk/nut milk
Spring or filtered water (optional)

How to prepare:

1. Take one banana's worth of frozen banana out of the freezer (chunks can be broken off with a blunt knife if you have a lot in there).

2. Roughly chop one fresh, ripe banana as well.

3. Place all ingredients into a blending jug, adding a cupful of rice milk (when I say cup here, just use about 200ml or so - but do experiment).

4. Blend together, **slowly** adding more rice milk or spring water to achieve desired thickness.

OK, so now you have the basics. Now the fun really starts!
What you can do is only really limited by your willingness to
explore, so give your creative juices full permission to flow.

See next page for suggestions...

SMOOTHIE SUGGESTIONS (IN NO PARTICULAR ORDER)

SUPERFOODS: Add a teaspoon of powdered (or freeze dried) superfoods or super-greens to the smoothie on blending. There are so many options out there these days. Some of my favourites are barley green powder, maca, lucama and acai berry powder.

OTHER FRUITS: If you have other fruits then add them to the blend in the place of the fresh banana (keep a fresh or frozen banana as a base for creaminess). Antioxidant rich berries and tropical fruits such as mango, papaya, pineapple and cherimoya tend to work particularly well.

INCREDIBLY DELICIOUS: Add a spoonful of tahini or almond butter. In our house, adding tahini is an absolute favourite. It is the secret "je ne sais quoi" of our smoothie world. Be warned though, it can be seriously addictive! Adding a little fat in this way can also slow down the release of the fruit sugar from the rest of the smoothie, giving you a more sustained boost of energy.

BANANA FREE: Banana is not compulsory! You might like to leave it out altogether and try something else. Use fresh or frozen fruit or a combination of both.

COCONUT SPECIAL: When in Hawaii, I love to put fresh coconut flesh in my smoothies. In England I opt for desiccated coconut instead – just a sprinkle, to give it a 'deluxe' sort of feeling. Desiccated coconut gives it an exciting 'chewy' effect.

BE TOTALLY LOCAL: If you happen to find yourself in a tropical place then you might be spoilt for choice for local fruits. You'll have to be a bit more creative to be totally local in a temperate climate, but be adventurous. During berry season we find wild blackberries in abundance at which point, they make a bountiful appearance in our breakfast cuisine.

GO GREEN: There's nothing like a bit of kale thrown in alongside your fruit for good measure. Experiment. Greens and fruit might not sound great, but it can really give it a vibrant feeling. Try one leaf at first. If you have a regular blender (rather than a top of the range one), make sure you destalk it and then chop as finely as you can before popping it in the blender.

GO SUPER GREEN: Nettles! A few tender young nettle leaves can pack a powerful boost of fresh superfood into your smoothie. The moisture will almost instantly denature the sting, so that you can enjoy all the benefits of raw nettle without getting stung.

APPLE AND CINNAMON: I love this rustic smoothie, especially when the weather is chilly. Chop up a ripe, unfrozen banana. Chop one large, sweet apple. Add them both into the blender jug, along with a heaped tablespoon of desiccated coconut, a level teaspoon of cinnamon and a heaped teaspoon of either tahini or organic almond butter. Add enough rice or coconut milk to rise to a little above the half way line of your ingredients. Blend to desired consistency and then drink or enjoy with a spoon.

FREEZE YOUR OTHER FRUIT: If you have berries or local fruits in season in abundance, then freeze them for smoothies. That means you can enjoy them over an extended period of time, long after the fruit season is over. Just take out the required amount as and when you need it and use any of the other suggestions here. The more frozen fruit you use, the thicker your smoothie will be; so consider adding some non-frozen fruit or liquid (vegan milk, fruit juice or water) to the blend.

NO FREEZE: So you don't have time to freeze your bananas? Just pop them in as they come.

LITTLE EXTRA FLAVOURS:
Try mint, ginger, lemon or lime
(not necessarily together) for bit of zing!
If in doubt, add a little at a time.

IMAGINATION:
Remember there is no limit to what you
can create if you give your creative
juices full permission to flow.

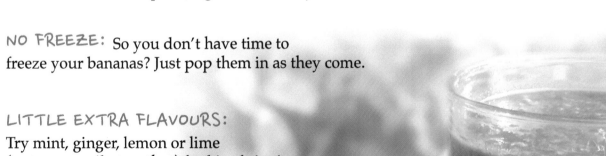

Good Morning Granola

A lovely, popular addition to breakfast if you need something filling. If you are sensitive to oats, then replace them with quinoa flakes instead. Granola keeps for weeks in an airtight container.

Preparation: 10 minutes
Cooking: 30 minutes (baked)/
10 minutes (grilled)

Ingredients:

500g rolled oats
100g seeds (sunflower or pumpkin etc.)
100g desiccated coconut
1 heaped tablespoon ground cinnamon
100ml olive oil
100ml date syrup
1 teaspoon almond essence

1. Mix all dried ingredients together in a large, deep edged, oven tray.

2. Add oil, syrup and almond essence to dried ingredients, mixing together thoroughly. Make sure that all of the oats are coated well with the mixture.

3. You can either bake this or grill it (see opposite).

4. You know that it is cooked when it is tanned all over.

5. Allow to cool, then serve with chopped fresh fruit, such as apple, banana or strawberries. Add a little nut or rice milk to moisten the granola.

GRILL: Place under a grill (medium heat) for up to 10 minutes. Stir mixture several times during the cooking period to ensure even, thorough cooking throughout. If you use pumpkin seeds - they might start to pop when the granola needs a bit of a stir.

BAKE: If you prefer baking (which I do), then bake at around gas mark 6 (200°C/400°F) for about 30 minutes. Stir several times throughout the cooking period so that it doesn't burn on top.

Serving suggestion:
Try adding raisins or chopped dried fruit to the mixture after it has been cooked.

MUESLI

I enjoyed my Mother's homemade muesli as a staple breakfast food when I was a youngster. It also happens to be a great way of sneaking some wholesome foods into the first meal of the day. Rather than giving a defined recipe, I thought it might be more helpful to list some ingredient suggestions. After all, conscious food creation is all about finding what works for you.

Ingredient suggestions:

Rolled oats or quinoa flakes
Coconut - shredded or desiccated
Seeds - sunflower, pumpkin, sesame
Nuts - hazelnuts, brazils, walnuts, almonds or cashews
Dried fruit - un-sulphured apricots, raisins, sultanas,
*   goji berries, dates, figs, mulberries*

Feel inspired and mix together a favourite blend. Let your intuition weave a little magic as you find ratios of different ingredients that work perfectly for you.

Make a whole batch and shake together in a sealed container or create a unique medley every time in your breakfast bowl.

Add fresh fruit and a dash of rice milk when you are ready to eat.

AVALON APPLE COMPOTE

Somerset, the county I live in, is full of apple orchards. So what to do when autumn comes and they are falling on my doorstep? The stewed apple compote has become a welcomed autumnal change to the breakfast menu in our house, especially when we have so many apples that we don't know what to do with them.

Serves: 2
Preparation: 3 minutes
Cooking: 4 minutes

Ingredients:
4 medium sized sweet apples
½ lemon juiced (or a splash of water)
½ teaspoon of mixed warming spices
(cinnamon, ginger, nutmeg)

1. Chop apple into 1cm cubes (roughly). Leave the skin on.
2. Juice lemon and compost the rind.
3. Place apples into a pan along with the freshly squeezed lemon juice and cook on a medium heat for approximately 4 minutes (longer if you want it really stewed). Stir with a wooden spoon throughout the cooking time to ensure even cooking.
4. Mix in the ground warming spices during the final minute.
5. Serve warm on its own or with a sprinkle of your favourite nuts and seeds, granola or muesli.

Alternatives:
Use pears instead of apples - or a blend of the two.
If you don't have lemon juice, just add 2 tablespoons of fresh water instead.

"Until he extends his circle of compassion
to include all living things,
man will not himself find peace."

~Albert Schweitzer~

MILLET & COCONUT PORRIDGE

When the colder months set in, I sometimes feel the need for something warm and filling for breakfast. I love regular oat porridge, although, being sensitive to oats, I find that it makes me feel tired and heavy. The answer is millet porridge! It's an alkalising food, with a myriad of nutrients. It contains serotonin, which is said to help against feeling depressed, whilst promoting relaxation and well being. Our serotonin levels often decline in the darker months, making millet a perfect winter 'feel good' breakfast. It's gluten free and easy to digest.

Serves: 1
Preparation: 2 minutes
Cooking: 12 minutes

Ingredients:

50g millet flakes or whole millet
200g water
200g coconut milk
1 tablespoon maple syrup
(or 1 small banana chopped)

1. Place millet and water in a pan and bring to the boil, stirring frequently with a wooden spoon.

2. Once all of the water has been absorbed (which can happen quickly) add the coconut milk and maple syrup (or banana).

3. If using banana, press in with spoon, to encourage it to permeate through the cooking porridge.

4. It should be fully cooked within 10 minutes after coming to the boil.

Alternatives:
Use rice or nut milk instead of coconut milk.
Try replacing the sweetener with medjool dates.

Date & Cinnamon Porridge

This is a real winner for those who love oats in the morning. I serve this during winter retreats, when our guests are looking for something warm and nurturing to start the day. For those who are intolerant to oats, try millet or quinoa flakes instead.

Serves: 1
Preparation: 5 minutes
Cooking: 10 minutes
(plus overnight soaking)

Ingredients:

(Quantities per person)
5 pitted dates
70g oats
Spring water
1 teaspoon ground cinnamon
Rice milk

The night before:

1. Chop dates and place in pan.

2. Add oats, along with enough spring water to fully submerge the oats, plus a little more. The oats will absorb all of this before morning light. Throughout the whole cooking process they tend to use up three parts liquid to one part oats (this includes the soak-water and then rice milk for cooking the next day).

3. Allowing the dates and oats to soak overnight softens them in advance, reducing the overall cooking time. This encourages a more gentle cooking process whilst saving energy.

Breakfast time:

1. Add the cinnamon and bring the contents of the pan to the boil, stirring in some rice milk (or water if you want it less creamy) as needed.

2. As the porridge cooks and thickens, add a little more rice milk at a time to achieve your desired consistency. Some people prefer it thick, some prefer it thinner.

3. Gently simmer on a low heat for five to ten minutes. When the dates begin to melt, press them in with a wooden spoon as you stir. They should begin to flood the porridge with delicious sweetness.

Notes:

If you didn't soak the oats and dates the night before, it still works fine to cook it in the morning. You will need to make sure the dates are chopped finely and you'll need to increase the cooking time accordingly.

ALL ABOUT COCONUTS

I fell in love with this sublime food after spending many moons in Hawaii. Drinking fresh coconut water and scooping out the soft, jelly like flesh from the husk is nothing short of a a heavenly experience. Botanically speaking , the coconut is a high vibrational, fatty fruit. It is found locally in more tropical climates, playing an important role in health wherever it is available.

Whilst I am a strong advocate of using whatever is local, I still find myself welcoming the gift of coconut, for now, when I am in the UK (which is most of the time). It has a pulse that lends itself so beautifully to higher consciousness. It is as if the coconut emits a frequency that awakens the soul to our divine origins.

Since it makes a rather avid appearance in the cooked dishes in this book, below, I've listed the main forms that you can purchase, to avoid any confusion:

CREAMED COCONUT BLOCK –

this is easily available in the UK in health food shops, oriental supermarkets and the ethnic sections of supermarkets. It comes in a solid block, somewhat like a bar of soap. This is the pure, dehydrated flesh of a mature coconut – creamed and compressed into a block. It can be stored at room temperature and melts upon heating. It has a rich coconut flavour and creates a thick velvety texture when melted into your cooking. We use it a lot in the conscious kitchen. This is always top of my shopping list for adding a little 'je ne sais quoi' to dishes.

FRESH COCONUT –

always my first choice if it is ever an option. Fresh coconut is harvested as a young, green fruit. Once the green shell is removed you get the familiar 'fairground' brown, hairy, husky looking thing. When young, the water is like a pranic nectar. The flesh is delectable.

COCONUT CREAM –

a thicker more potent version of the coconut milk. Perhaps the best substitute for creamed coconut block.

COCONUT MILK –

this can vary enormously in quality and taste. Contrary to popular belief, the milk of coconut milk, isn't the liquid that you pour from the fresh coconut. It is the liquid gained from pressing from the grated coconut meat as well as the coconut water. It tends to come in a can or a carton. Personally, I almost always opt for creamed coconut block before coconut milk, preferring its ultra rich creaminess and highly aromatic fragrance, when melted in the pot. Always choose a high quality variety.

COCONUT OIL –

a great addition to conscious cuisine. This is the oil extracted from coconut meat. Oil quality can vary greatly. I recommend extra virgin or cold pressed, organic coconut oil. It solidifies below 24°C (76°F). To melt it, place your bottle on a warmed windowsill or near something that will raise it's temperature gently. It also happens to be one of the best choices when it comes to heating oils, as it remains stable at high temperatures for longer than most oils (which damages the oil less).

Always buy coconut consciously. Look for organic, fairly traded and sustainable options. The rising demand for coconut means that we should really keep our ear to the ground on the ethics of coconut production. Mass demand often skews ethics. The best option by far of course, if you live in the tropics, is to embrace your local delights.

DESICCATED COCONUT – this is shredded or flaked coconut with the moisture taken out. It can vary from country to country. Use unsweetened, organic varieties.

COCONUT SUGAR – is taken from the sap of the coconut flower, which, sadly means that the tree will never produce a coconut from that blossom. However, if it is consciously obtained from sustainable sources, then you'll enjoy the benefits from copious amounts of nutrients, as well as having a healthful sweetener that is low on the glycemic index.

Salads

Salads can work cosmic wonders for our energetic vibration. They are usually the main food choice in our Conscious Kitchen. We adore big, full, prana-packed salads, brimming with life force as main meals, rather than 'side dish' add ons.

We enjoy them for lunch with pâtés and dips. We equally adore them for dinner, along with a warming side dish such as mushroom millet, seed loaf, falafels, quinoa or hempy potatoes.

The secret to a good salad is a good salad dressing. The amazing thing is that there are so many different combinations that you really could have a different one every day of the year. In this section, I've listed a few of our favourites. But remember, the limit is your imagination!

Cosmic Carrot & Ginger Salad

A delicious, tangy salad with carrot, sundried tomatoes and ginger.

Serves: 4
Preparation: 15 minutes
(plus overnight soaking)

Ingredients:

Three medium/large carrots grated
Sundried tomato dressing (below)

Dressing ingredients:

1 teaspoon (heaped) fresh ginger
1 handful (50g) chopped sundried tomatoes
3 tablespoons apple cider vinegar
75ml cold pressed sunflower oil
2 teaspoons apple juice concentrate

This is quick to make, although it is best to prepare the dressing the evening before.

1. Grate the peeled ginger with a fine grater (in a bowl, so that you don't lose the ginger juice).

2. Place all dressing ingredients in a bowl or jug together.

3. Gently mix together and then leave for a minimum of two hours to infuse. The longer the better.

4. When the dressing is ready (the sundried tomatoes have softened) mix in with the grated carrot.

Serving suggestions:

Serve with grain such as rice/millet/quinoa or potato to make a vibrant filling main meal. Or serve as part of a lighter lunch with salad leaves and hummus.

CAULIFLOWER & TAHINI SALAD

A thick, creamy, nutritious dish that serves delightfully well as part of a salad buffet.

Serves: 4
Preparation time: 15 minutes

Ingredients:

1 small/medium cauliflower
Cashew or hazelnuts (small handful)
Cauliflower greens
Tahini sauce

Tahini sauce ingredients:

⅓ jar tahini (100g approx)
1 tablespoon apple cider vinegar
1 tablespoon apple juice concentrate
1 tablespoon tamari/shoyu
25 – 50ml water

1. Mix the tahini sauce by putting all its ingredients (with only about 25ml of water) in a bowl. You might have to be quite persistent with the tahini – it can be a bit stubborn! It will turn rewardingly creamy if you keep at it. Add a little extra water at a time if you need more liquid. You are looking for a thick cream consistency.

2. Chop the cauliflower lovingly, to retain some of the florets.

3. If the cauliflower comes with some nice delicate greens then toss them in along with the nuts (the outer ones are normally too tough for salad).

4. Mix together thoroughly with the tahini sauce, until everything is coated. If the sauce thickens too much whilst mixing, then add a dash of water to loosen it again.

Variation:

Feel free to add other things in with this e.g. a few freshly chopped tomatoes, some chopped lettuce or kale.

THE RAWSOME MIX

The rawsome mix is a versatile salad dish, that has evolved, grown and taken on many different forms over the years. It's a finely chopped salad, evoking an incredible poetic frolic of flavours to excite the taste buds. This version here is one of our more typical blends, usually created by my lovely, kitchen friendly husband. This works best if you can finely chop everything. It works particularly well if you use a hand food processor to do the work for you, chopping everything ever finer to encourage a delightful blend.

Serves: 2
Preparation: 10 minutes

Ingredients:

1 small head of broccoli
1 medium carrot
1 small red pepper
1 medium sized apple
½ small onion
1 small - medium ripe avocado
1 heaped teaspoon mustard from a jar
1 tablespoon tamari
1 tablespoon apple cider vinegar
2 tablespoons olive oil
1 teaspoon apple juice concentrate

1. Grate carrot and finely chop all other ingredients.
2. Put all ingredients in a bowl together and mix thoroughly with a spoon. Alternatively, use a hand food processor.

EARTH CHAKRA RAINBOW FEAST

A rainbow feast for the earthly chakras. Green leaves and celery for the heart; yellow pepper and pine nuts for the solar plexus; carrots for the sacrum and tomatoes and red pepper for the base chakra. Colours can affect our consciousness, so allow this rainbow feast of colours to bathe and nurture your earthly chakras.

Serves: 3
Preparation: 10 minutes

Ingredients:

1 small yellow bell pepper
1 small red bell pepper
2 large kale leaves
2 medium carrots
1 celery stalk
2 medium tomatoes
Handful pine nuts
A few sprigs of parsley
1 tablespoon hemp oil
½ tablespoon apple cider vinegar
½ lemon juiced
Dash of tamari to taste
Handful of green olives

1. Chop the peppers, carrots and celery into small squares.
2. Slice tomatoes.
3. Slice kale into small pieces.
4. Mix chopped vegetables and olives together in a bowl with oil, vinegar and tamari.
5. Sprinkle parsley leaves and pine nuts on top.

Variation:

Use brazil nuts or cashews instead of pine nuts.

Homemade Pesto Salad

An absolutely delicious, easy way to enjoy your homemade pesto in abundance.

Serves: 1
Preparation: 10 minutes

Ingredients:

½ small broccoli
Generous helping of greens
  (i.e. kale, rocket)
4 cherry tomatoes
¼ apple
1 heaped tablespoon of homemade pesto
  (see page 74)
A little olive oil and lemon

1. Cut the tough bits off the broccoli stalk, then chop rest of the broccoli and tender stalk into small pieces. This can be either very fine or coarse depending on your personal preference.

2. Roughly chop greens and cut tomatoes into quarters.

3. Finely chop apple into small pieces.

4. Toss everything in a salad bowl and mix in with the pesto (adding an extra drizzle of olive oil and a squeeze of lemon juice to loosen the pesto up if needed).

Serving suggestion:

This serves nicely with other salads, as a meal on it's own or with a side dish of rice, quinoa or potatoes.

CURRIED CHICKPEAS

A protein crammed platter for those who enjoy a more fiery cuisine.

Serves: 2 to 4
Preparation: 10 minutes

Ingredients:

2 tins chickpeas (approx 500g drained)
1 level teaspoon medium curry powder
25g raisins
1 tablespoon olive oil
2 teaspoons apple cider vinegar
1 teaspoon apple juice concentrate
2 teaspoons shoyu
Loose handful of fresh coriander
Small sweet red pepper or a few
cherry tomatoes (optional extras)

1. Thoroughly rinse and drain the chickpeas and place in a salad bowl.

2. Mix in raisins and curry powder.

3. Add oil, vinegar, apple juice concentrate and shoyu thoroughly.

4. Gently tear the herbs.

5. Chop and toss in herbs along with any chopped optional extras.

6. Enjoy!

Serving suggestion:

This serves as an interesting addition to a salad buffet or as a side dish with rice or barley.

Notes: If you start with dried chickpeas, soaking and cooking your own from scratch (as I do rather than buying them precooked), then 250g dried should yield a little more than 500g. The final yield does vary from batch to batch though, so it's hard to pin down the exact measurements. I usually take advantage of the energy I am using to cook and boil up a whole panful to add into other dishes during the week.

Herbs such as parsley or basil work well as an alternative to coriander in this dish.

Ascension Salad

If there was just one salad that I ever ate, it would be the 'Ascension Salad'. In essence, it is a super-green, nutrient dense, high energy meal, perfectly suited to raising our vibration. The health benefits of each individual food item could easily take up a book in itself, so I'll just list a brief overview of each one. If you are interested, I urge you to explore further and find out more about these foods. I find that eating this type of salad on a daily basis has really helped to raise my vibration, proving to be a powerful catalyst on my journey of spiritual unfolding. It has ensured that I maintain an optimal level of health.

I've listed my favourite 'Ascension Salad' ingredients below. Go with the proportions that best suit yourself. Lovingly chop, tear or toss into a salad bowl and then drizzle with hemp oil and freshly juiced lemon or lime and enjoy either on its own or alongside a raw pâté or dip.

KALE – loaded with vitamins, minerals and antioxidants. Kale has a long list of health benefits. It is a must in any conscious cuisine.

ROCKET – another nutrient rich green, with a delicious peppery flavour.

AVOCADO – the perfect way to get a super-hit of essential fats and protein.

CORIANDER LEAVES – a herb considered to have a myriad of health benefits including cleansing of the heavy metals that we all seem to be exposed to in our environment these days.

DANDELION GREENS – excellent cleansing properties. Can be bitter, so try the youngest, freshest leaves first.

CELERY – containing a plethora of antioxidants, high in calcium and has a beneficial alkalising effect. I like to add this to my salad for a nice crunch.

COLD PRESSED HEMP OIL – with the perfect 3:1 balance of Omega-6 and Omega-3 essential fatty acids, this is said to be an amazing oil for optimum health. It is my number one choice when it comes to oil.

LEMON OR LIME – freshly juiced lemon has a great alkalising effect on the body. It has also been shown to have a hidden catalogue of health benefits including anti-bacterial, anti-viral, liver cleansing properties. I find a bit of zing goes nicely with a salad.

AVALON AUTUMN CRUNCH

Whenever I think of walnuts, I think of my dear friend Fiona gathering them when they'd fallen from a tree here one Avalonian autumn. There are so many things that we can forage in our neighbourhood when we start looking closer. This type of blend really excites me, because I can create it almost totally out of ingredients that I forage, grow or buy from local sources.

Serves: 2
Preparation: 10 minutes

Ingredients:

75g walnuts
1½ tablespoons hemp oil
1 small or medium apple
3 large romaine leaves
¼ small red cabbage
¼ small onion (optional)
1 tablespoon apple cider vinegar
1 teaspoon apple juice concentrate
2 teaspoons shoyu

1. Chop the apple into small cubes.

2. Chop or sliver the cabbage and lettuce how ever you prefer.

3. Finely chop the onion if you are opting for it.

4. Mix all chopped ingredients into a bowl along with the walnuts, apple cider vinegar, apple juice concentrate and shoyu.

"*Every thought you produce,*
anything you say,
any action you do,
bears your signature."

~Thich Nhat Hanh~

St Francis Basil & Avo Salad

St Francis, the saint of true compassion, is very close to my heart. Not in a religious sense, but from the essence of his energy, where we all connect soul to soul, as one. The St Francis Salad, is a favourite blend of mine, inspired by a well-rounded, compassionate diet of tasty plant foods.

Serves: 2
Preparation: 10 minutes

Ingredients:

A few kale leaves
Large handful of fresh basil
½ sweet juicy apple
Medium sized ripe avocado
Handful of cherry tomatoes
Handful of mizuna leaves
One small carrot
1 tablespoon hemp oil
Dash of apple cider vinegar
Dash of tamari

1. Take off any tough kale stalks (if they aren't tough, then leave them in) and chop kale into bite sizes.

2. Grate or chop carrot.

3. Roughly tear mizuna leaves.

4. Chop apple into small cubes, leaving on the skin.

5. Chop the cherry tomatoes into halves.

6. Chop the avocado in half, take out the stone, score the avocado flesh into cubes before scooping out with a spoon.

7. Mix everything together, dressing with hemp oil, apple cider vinegar and tamari at the same time as tossing in the whole basil leaves.

Notes: Mizuna is a leaf that is gaining increasing popularity. If your can't find it locally try finding some seeds and growing your own. Rocket is a great alternative to mizuna.

St Francis has infused an unmistakable shining
light here amongst us; a message that ALL beings
are worthy of love and compassion; a message that
the strength of true compassion is enough to shatter
the old world and unleash the light of the earth to
birth a new one - a new world based on unconditional love and compassion for all. His message has
come in many forms, encoded in the space between
the spaces, as a story free from dogma, to be touched
only by the Soul. It carries with it an untainted
innocence waiting to be realised and reborn. The message awaits within the heart of each of us, dormant
until stirred, like a hibernating seed, unaware,
yet ever yearning for the moment to be set free.

The gift that St Francis brings us holds an
important key to human evolution...
'compassion for all sentient life'.

MINTY CUCUMBER SALAD

A perfect cooling salad for a hot summers day.

Serves: 4 portions
Preparation: 10 minutes

Ingredients:

1 large cucumber
Mint sauce

Mint sauce ingredients:
1 large handful fresh garden mint
Pinch sea salt
3 tablespoons apple cider vinegar
3 tablespoons olive oil
½ medium sized apple

1. Chop cucumber into slices or cubes. I tend to chop them into 1cm cubes, although it's a matter of choice. Place chopped cucumber in a bowl ready for the mint sauce.
2. Leave the skin on the apple and chop into small chunks.
3. Place the de-stalked mint leaves, chopped apple and all remaining mint sauce ingredients in a jug and blend with a hand blender to create a thick mint sauce.
4. Mix the mint sauce in with the cucumber. Garnish with some fresh mint leaves and serve fresh along with another salad.

Sprouted Quinoa & Shiitake Salad

A living, breathing, vibrant gift from heaven.

Serves: 2
Preparation: 10 minutes, plus
1 to 3 days to sprout quinoa.

Ingredients:

*100g sprouted quinoa
(see page 57 for quinoa sprouts)
1 ripe avocado
½ stick of celery
A few little pieces of soaked sundried tomato
A tiny sprinkle of raisins
A small handful of rocket
4 tablespoons of 'Shakti Shiitake
& Sesame dressing' (see page 76)*

1. Slice and cut avocado into smallish cubes.

2. Slice celery thinly.

3. Mix all ingredients together and let the flavours flood your taste buds.

Alternatives:

If you don't have time to make the shiitake dressing, then you can whip up an alternative in no time. Add: *1 teaspoon of toasted sesame oil, 1 teaspoon tamari, 1 tablespoon of apple cider vinegar and 2 tablespoons of sunflower oil* (or something similar) to the final mix instead.

Vegan-Slaw

A tasty, conscious alternative to coleslaw.

Serves: 4
Preparation: 20 minutes

Ingredients:

*½ a small white cabbage
2 large carrots
1 medium onion*

Tahini sauce:

*Use tahini sauce recipe (page 66)
using same quantity
Ground mustard 1 teaspoon (optional)*

1. Grate the cabbage and carrots.

2. Finely chop the onion.

3. Mix mustard into the tahini sauce.

4. Mix everything together thoroughly.

Serving suggestion:
Serve alongside a leafy green salad with potato wedges.

Grow Your Own Salad Sprouts

Every conscious kitchen should have salad sprouts on the go. Sprouting seeds is an excellent way of having year round, fresh, local produce for salad. Soaking seeds releases the enzyme inhibitors, making them very easy to digest. With a little TLC, they will go on to produce copious amounts of power packed, edible shoots. All good health food shops stock seeds for sprouting these days. They are easily available to purchase in bulk online too. You can buy sprouting kits and trays, although I've always just used what was available to hand.

Sprouting Alfalfa, Broccoli and Clover Seeds

This method works specifically with seeds such as alfalfa, broccoli and clover sprouts. You can sprout them as a mix together or as a single seed.

STEP ONE: Place a large handful of seeds in large jar. I use a two litre jar. If you have a smaller jar then experiment with fewer seeds.

STEP TWO: Soak the seeds for at least six hours (I usually leave them to soak overnight), using spring or filtered water.

STEP THREE: After soaking, place muslin (or fine mesh) over the top of the jar and hold securely in place with an elastic band. Drain off the soak-water and rinse until the water is clear.

STEP FOUR: Allow any excess water to drain from the jar by tilting upside down at an angle (I leave it on my dish draining rack for a half hour or so). Keep the jar in a light airy place in the kitchen or utility room.

STEP FIVE: Rinse sprouting seeds through and drain as in step four, at least once per day (in warm weather consider rinsing twice a day).

STEP SIX: The sprouts should be ready in about five or six days time when you begin to see green tips on the ends. At this point you need to remove the brown husks. Empty contents of jar into a large bowl. Fill with water until almost full. Agitate and shake the water to make the husks rise to the surface. Spoon out the husks or splash over the edge into the sink (losing a few sprouts is unavoidable). Scoop out the sprouts by hand and put into a sieve. Tip out any husks that remain in the bottom of the bowl along with the waste water. Rinse out the bowl, put the sprouting seeds back into the bowl, fill with water and repeat (agitate, scoop etc.) removing as many husks as possible. Allow your remaining sprouts to drain free of water through a sieve.

STEP SEVEN: Store in a sealed container in the fridge and they should last for a good five days (tip: if they are not sufficiently drained of water they will go soggy, so make sure you drain them well).

Sprouting Quinoa

Step One: Quinoa has a soapy saponin coating that must be rinsed off prior to soaking. Sometimes it has been done for you before purchasing. Rinse just in case.

Step Two: Soak for approximately half an hour - longer is fine if you forget.

Step Three: Rinse and drain thoroughly with sieve and leave in either a sprouting jar or a bowl between 8 and 12 hours.

Step Four: Repeat step three at least one more time for a maximum of three days.

They will start to sprout within a day and are usable as soon as you want them. That might be after one day or several. The texture changes depending on the sprouting time, so find the duration that works best for you.

The secret is to make sure that you drain them thoroughly. The single, most common reason for sprouting disasters is not draining them sufficiently.

Sprouting Sunflower Seeds

Black sunflower seeds are the most reliable for sprouting. Not only do these work well in a salad, they are also a superb, munch-able snack.

Step One: Soak seeds in a jar for anywhere between 8 - 24 hours.

Step Two: Place a layer of compost/soil about 1 to 3cm deep in a seed tray.

Step Three: Spread your soaked sunflower seeds evenly over the layer of soil. The best way to do this, is to have no soil showing, spreading seeds one sunflower seed thick.

Step Four: Cover the tray with a seed tray or cloth (to stop the soil and seeds drying out) for about four days. Water very lightly (or use a light plant mister to spray) daily if needed, to keep the seeds moist.

Step Five: After four days remove the cover. A semi-shaded room is fine for their growth from this stage onwards. Your seeds should be well on their way to growing by now. Allow them to continue to grow, watering daily as necessary.

Step Six: They are ready to eat once some are beginning to grow a second set of leaves (about 10 - 12 days). Snip them off as low down the stem as you can and enjoy them in abundance with salad.

Dressings & Dips

Conscious Kitchen pâtés and dips are an invaluable addition to any healthy cuisine. They are small, super condensed portions of highly nutritious, protein filled vitality. They offer the perfect opportunity to jazz things up, making salads, wraps and sandwiches decidedly more interesting. Great dressings can really transform a salad, so I encourage you to get creative with your own favourite ingredients, oils and things. It's a sure approach to making eating consciously so delicious, that you couldn't imagine eating any other way. I hope that some of the suggestions here will encourage you to find blends that work wonders for you.

"I have come into the world to see this:
the sword drop from mens hands
even at the height of their arc of rage,
because we have finally realized
there is just one flesh we can wound."

~Hafiz~

Heavenly Hummus

Life just wouldn't be the same without hummus dip.
Add sundried tomatoes for a delicious variation.

Serves: 6
Preparation: 15 minutes

Ingredients:

500g cooked chickpeas
  (approx 2 tins drained)
2 medium lemons
1 large garlic clove
4 tablespoons tahini
8 tablespoons olive oil or sunflower oil
4 tablespoons tamari or shoyu
Spring water (approx 100ml)

1. Drain and thoroughly rinse chickpeas.
2. Juice lemons and toss skins in the compost.
3. Finely chop or crush garlic.
4. Place all ingredients in blender and blend until creamy and smooth.
5. Refrigerate before serving.

Notes: This should keep for up to a week although it will thicken upon refrigerating. If you'd like to thin it down, then simply add a dash of water and mix in.

Sun Garden Pâté

We use soaked seeds as the base for the sun garden pâté. Soaking living seeds unleashes their enzyme inhibitors to bring forth an even more powerful infusion of life force.

Serves: 4
Preparation: 15 minutes
(plus overnight soaking)

Ingredients:

100g sunflower seeds
1 medium carrot grated
2 heaped tablespoons fresh parsley
1 heaped teaspoon rosemary & thyme
1 clove garlic (medium)
¼ small onion
2 teaspoons shoyu
½ lemon
Spring water to soak seeds

1. Soak sunflower seeds overnight (or for at least 3 hours) in water. They will start to swell by absorbing the water, whilst beginning to unleash their life force.

2. Juice lemon and discard the rind.

3. Grate carrot.

4. Chop herbs finely.

5. Crush garlic and finely chop onion.

6. Drain the soak-water from the seeds and place in a jug for blending.

7. Place all ingredients in a jug and blend. It's generally easiest with a hand blender, applying a bit of downward pressure with your first few pulsations, clearing the blade, if it gets stuck.

English Garden Pâté

English garden pâté is a filling, super healthy, sunflower seed pâté made from things that would 'mostly' be available in any good kitchen garden in a temperate climate.

Serves: 3 - 5
Preparation: 15 minutes

Ingredients:

150g sunflower seeds
1 medium carrot grated
1 heaped tablespoon parsley,
rosemary, lemon thyme
1 clove garlic (medium)
½ teaspoon celtic sea salt
1 teaspoon concentrated
 apple juice
A little spring water to bind

1. Grind your shelled sunflower seeds in a nut mill or coffee grinder (or alternatively, crush using a pestle and mortar by hand).

2. Grate carrot.

3. Chop herbs finely.

4. Crush garlic.

5. Place all ingredients together in a large mixing bowl and mix together.

6. Add a little water at a time until you acquire the pâté consistency that you prefer.

7. Allow the flavours to dance together for a few hours if you have time or serve immediately.

Notes:

This pâté is best served fresh. It will oxidise on the surface if left for any period of time. This is perfectly normal. If you make it for serving later, simply stir in with a spoon before serving.

Tahini Sauce

Tahini can really save the day if you are looking for a rich creamy and ever-so-satiating addition to a salad. This sauce is an excellent dressing, especially for more dense ingredients such as raw cauliflower.

Ingredients:

100g tahini
1 tablespoon apple cider vinegar (or lemon juice)
1 tablespoon apple juice concentrate
1 tablespoon tamari/shoyu
50ml water

1. Add all ingredients together and mix thoroughly until creamy, adding the water a little at a time.

2. Be persistent with the tahini – sometimes it takes a little while to get the drift of what you are doing.

3. If the sauce thickens too much add more water a little at a time to achieve desired consistency.

Serving suggestion:

This serves tastefully well as a dressing for dense, raw vegetables, such as cauliflower, carrot, sweet potato, cabbage or swede.

Sweetini Pâté (sweet potato & tahini)

This is ideal if you suddenly need to make a pâté with very little time to hand. It works nicely with salad and rice cakes, homemade oatcakes or other crackers. These quantities are approximate and can be varied a little.

Serves: 3
Preparation: 10 minutes

Ingredients:

One small sweet potato
100g of tahini
1 tablespoon lemon juice or apple cider vinegar
1 teaspoon apple juice concentrate
1 teaspoon tamari/shoyu
2 tablespoons spring water

1. Peel and grate sweet potato.

2. Mix everything together in a bowl, with a spoon until you achieve a pâté type consistency. It may help to use a teaspoon to keep scraping the coagulating tahini mixture from the spoon.

Sundried Tomato & Nettle Pâté

I first served this one during a surprise picnic that I'd prepared for my husband. We just sat there and said 'WOW! This is so good', with every mouthful. The nettles give it a vibrant hit of Mother Nature's superfood, whilst the other ingredients infuse into a delectable chorus of flavours.

Serves: 4 - 6
Preparation: 15 minutes
(plus overnight soaking)

Ingredients:

100g sundried tomatoes (still dried)
Spring water to soak
1 small onion
40g nettle leaves (destalked)
  (one large compact handful)
6 tablespoons olive oil
2 teaspoons shoyu
4 tablespoons of water
  (use left over soak-water).

1. Soak a large handful of sundried tomatoes overnight in water and drain off the soak-water into a cup the next day.

2. Finely chop onion.

3. Using rubber gloves, roughly chop the nettles (which should be without the stalks at this stage).

4. Add 4 tablespoons of soak-water, along with the olive oil, shoyu and ½ of the of chopped nettles.

5. This blends best with a hand blender or a food processor. Pulsate to blend, clearing the blade regularly until it starts to combine. Add the rest of the nettles a little at a time. Blend until you achieve a rustic, 'spreadable' effect.

Serving suggestion:

We relish this with salad, oatcakes, crackers or even use as a topping for a raw pizza. It works beautifully as part of a wrap or a sandwich.

Read more about nettles on page 119.

SUNDRIED TOMATO TAPENADE

An exciting way to use olives to make a scrumptious pâté.

Serves: 4 - 6
Preparation: 5 minutes
(plus overnight soaking)

Ingredients:

200g green or black pitted olives
40g sundried tomatoes
1 medium clove garlic
1 tablespoon olive oil

1. Soak sundried tomatoes overnight and then drain off the soak-water. If you use pre-soaked sundried tomatoes you will need about 80g of them rather than 40g.

2. Blend together well with a hand blender to make a pâté.

BASIL TAPENADE

An ultra fast way to make gourmet pâté, over flowing with tasty Mediterranean flavours.

Serves: 4
Preparation: 5 minutes

Ingredients:
50g fresh basil leaves
150g green olives
1 medium garlic clove
2 tablespoons olive oil

1. Crush garlic.

2. Place about ⅓ of the basil in a jug along with the other ingredients. Pulsate to break down the mixture with a hand blender. Add the remaining basil gradually whilst blending.

3. Clear the blade if it gets stuck. Pulsate and blend until you achieve a pâté consistency.

Basil-Moli

This recipe is a simple blend of flavours that make for a rather exquisite dip. The basil and avocado complement one another so perfectly. I enjoy this with a plate of salad. To be honest, I could quite happily live entirely on avocados if I lived in a country where they grow. This is one fatty fruit that I never, ever tire of.

Ingredients:

One ripe avocado
Handful fresh basil leaves
Squeeze of lemon
Dash of tamari/shoyu to taste

1. Make sure the avocado is really ripe. If it 'gives' nicely when you press with your fingers, it is ready.

2. Scoop out the avocado butter into a bowl. Mash with fork.

3. Roughly chop the basil leaves and mix in along with lemon and tamari.

4. Take a deep breath and let the delectable energies of avocado take you to ever higher realms of consciousness.

Coriander Guacamole

Coriander has a myriad of health benefits, not least, the uncanny ability to help remove heavy metals from our toxic bodies. In this day and age, we could use all the help we can get. I make a definite point of including this invaluable herb in our diet regularly. Mix it with avocado and you have a marriage made in heaven.

Ingredients:

One ripe avocado
Small handful of fresh coriander leaves
Dash of balsamic vinegar
Dash of tamari
Pinch of black pepper to taste

1. Make sure the avocado is really ripe. If it 'gives' nicely when you press with your fingers, it is ready.

2. Scoop out the avocado butter into a bowl. Mash with fork.

3. Roughly chop the coriander leaves and mix into avocado with the balsamic vinegar and tamari.

4. Serve immediately with salad or brown rice and tortilla wraps.

Wild Garlic & Walnut Pesto

Wild garlic is a spring time foraging speciality in Europe and Asia. This is a welcome addition to the salad table at a time of year when other greens are often a little lacking. The wild garlic I am using here is *Allium ursinum* also know as "ramsons" (as shown in flower in May time, in the image on this page). It's not to be confused with the *Allium vineale* variety of wild garlic also known as "crow garlic" more commonly found in North America and Australia.

Ingredients:

50g walnuts
½ lemon juiced
2 tablespoons olive oil
25g ramson leaves (wild garlic)
Pinch of sea salt

1. Put everything in a jug and blend, until you get a nice consistency. It's easier to blend with a hand blender, so that you can apply extra pressure to assist the process and easily clear the blade, if it gets stuck on the first few pulsations.

2. The flavour matures if you manage to keep this for a few days in the fridge without eating it all.

Variation:

Use 50g of sunflower seeds instead of walnuts, but soak them for at least an hour ahead of time, to soften them for blending. When ready, drain off the water and follow the same instructions as above.

Raw Pesto
(Sunflower seed and tamari version)

Soaking sunflower seeds is an excellent way to make them blendable. It also has the additional benefit of releasing the enzyme inhibitors within them, making them much more digestible. I certainly feel incredibly vibrant when I eat seeds, especially soaked ones. This is a tasty alternative to traditional Italian pesto.

Ingredients:

50g sunflower seeds
1 medium garlic clove
2 teaspoons tamari or shoyu
2 tablespoons olive oil
½ lemon
35g fresh basil leaves
Spring water to soak

Night before:

Soak sunflower seeds in at least twice as much water overnight. If you forget or feel spontaneous, then soaking for at least an hour will work fine too. A few hours is best, if you can, to allow time to absorb more water and unleash their vibrancy.

Next day:

1. Crush or finely chop garlic and juice lemon.

2. Add all ingredients (but only half of the basil) into a jug for blending.

3. Pulsate the blender, stopping to scrape the ingredients off the blade if it gets stuck.

4. Whilst blending, add rest of the basil a bit at a time.

5. This keeps in a jar for a few days, although the sunflower seed might oxidise a little (turning the pesto slightly brown on the edges) – if this happens, give it a quick mix with a teaspoon and it'll be right as rain!

Alternative to using a blender:

It really can feel good to make this without a blender too. Traditionally it would have been made with a pestle and mortar. If you feel inspired, you might like to try creating it the traditional way. It's an excellent way to connect with your food creation every step of the way.

Raw Hazelnut Pesto

There are so many hazelnut trees in the UK - perhaps if you are really keen, this will inspire you to gather your own nuts in the autumn, for a super high vibrational delicacy. This pesto tastes different to the sunflower seed and tamari version. The lemon, basil and garlic entwine together to achieve a deliciously arousing 'zinginess'.

Ingredients:

100g hazelnuts
Spring water (to soak hazelnuts)
½ large lemon
1 teaspoon finely grated lemon rind
1 medium garlic clove
6 tablespoons olive oil
Pinch of sea salt (or to preferred taste)
1 teaspoon balsamic vinegar
50g fresh basil (chopped)

Night before:

Soak hazelnuts in spring or filtered water overnight. Use enough to more than cover them – they will expand and soak up some of the water.

Next day:

1. Juice lemon and grate a teaspoon worth of rind.

2. Put everything in a blending jug except for the basil. Give it a few pulses with the blender and then start adding basil leaves a little at a time.

3. Keep pulsing blender until everything is evenly mixed together. A few rustic chunks here and there add nicely to the final effect.

4. Enjoy with salad or wheat-free pasta to your heart's delight.

Shakti & Shiitake Mushroom Dressing

Shakti represents the personification of the sacred divine feminine energy of the universe. When I first created this, I felt the primordial energy of Shakti rising through me to weave a powerful fusion of flavours. It's a tasty dressing that blends well with quinoa (cooked or sprouted), rice, wheat-free spaghetti or raw veggies.

Makes: 250 ml (about 1 cup)
Preparation: 10 minutes
(plus soak time)

Ingredients:

7 dried organic shiitake mushrooms
 (or one small handful)
1 tablespoon toasted sesame oil
6 tablespoons sunflower oil
3 tablespoons apple cider vinegar
1 tablespoon tamari
3 tablespoons water

1. If your mushrooms are whole, tear them up roughly first.

2. Add mushrooms with all remaining ingredients into a jug and leave to soak overnight (or for at least a couple of hours if you don't have time).

3. When soaked, blend together with a blender (a few speckles are fine - adding quite nicely to creativity).

4. Pour into a glass bottle and keep in the fridge for up to one week, using as required.

Galactic Garlic Salad Dressing

This is a thick creamy dressing that goes well with just about any of your spur of the moment 'whatever is in the fridge' kind of salads. So easy to whip up.

Serves: Several salads
Preparation: 5 minutes

Ingredients:

2 garlic cloves
150ml olive oil
1 tablespoon fresh parsley
50ml balsamic vinegar
Pinch of sea salt
1 teaspoon apple juice concentrate

1. Measure oil and vinegar into a glass jug.

2. Peel and crush garlic cloves and pop them into the jug with oil and vinegar.

3. Drop in fresh parsley leaves.

4. Blend for a few seconds with a hand blender. This should rapidly turn into a thick delicious sauce.

5. Store in a glass container and refrigerate for up to a week and use as needed or serve immediately.

"Humankind has not woven the web of life.
We are but one thread within it.
Whatever we do to the web, we do to ourselves.
All things are bound together.
All things connect."

~Chief Seattle~

Garden Herb Salad Dressing

Few things bring me as much joy as gathering fresh herbs from my garden or windowsill. The garden herb dressing is a flavoursome interweave of garden flavours, with a lovely hint of mustard.

Serves: A few salads
Preparation: 5 minutes

Ingredients:

1 clove garlic
150ml sunflower oil
75ml apple cider vinegar
1 teaspoon apple juice concentrate
1 heaped teaspoon mustard
(the ready made type in a jar)
1 heaped tablespoon herbs
(i.e. oregano, parsley, lemon thyme –
whatever is available or to your preference)
½ teaspoon celtic sea salt

1. Crush or finely chop garlic.

2. Blend all ingredients together.

3. Place mixture into a glass jar and either refrigerate or serve immediately. There is enough for several salads. It should last for a week or two if chilled. The flavour will also mature as it sits.

Tamari & Ginger Vinaigrette

This dressing is a zippy union of flavours, with a delicate hint of ginger. It works with most salads, yielding enough for a good few portions.

Serves: A few salads worth
Preparation: 5 minutes

Ingredients:

1cm cube peeled ginger
1 small garlic clove
4 tablespoons sunflower oil
2 tablespoons apple cider vinegar
1 tablespoon tamari
1 tablespoon apple juice concentrate

1. Finely chop ginger and garlic.

2. Toss all ingredients into a jug and blend until smooth. If you don't have a blender available, just crush and grate the ginger very finely, then mix, shake and share.

3. Serve immediately mixed into your salad or put it in a glass bottle to keep for a week or two.

Soups

Soups are a bit of an all round winner. They tend to be quick and easy to make for a group of people and often taste even better when they are reheated for the second time. As with everything in this book, they offer an opportunity to create a dish consciously, infusing healthy, hearty, nutritious foods into your meal. In our home we welcome them on cold winter evenings with flat bread or heart shaped oatcakes.

Trin's Soul Food Special

The title might give the game away here. This is indeed, one of my all time favourite soups. It's an aromatic, colourful medley of ingredients that just want to be in the pan together! The sweet potato will fall apart, infusing with the coconut, to create a delightful velvety texture.

Serves: 4
Preparation time: 15 minutes
Cooking time: 30 minutes

Ingredients:

25g–50g dried shiitake mushrooms
4 small-medium sweet potatoes (1kg)
1 bottle unsalted passata (700g approx)
Nettle (4 large handfuls)
 or kale (few large leaves)
100g creamed coconut block (or see
below for coconut cream alternative)
1 teaspoon sea salt
1 litre spring water (approx)

1. Pre-soak the mushrooms for a few hours or overnight using enough of the spring water to cover them all. If you forget this bit or just fancy this soup on the spur of the moment and don't have time, then it still works - but tear the mushrooms into quite small pieces first and then follow the instructions below.

2. When you are ready to start making the soup bring the mushrooms to the boil (in the soak-water) and allow to cook for up to 10 minutes whilst preparing the rest of the ingredients.

3. Chop sweet potato, with skin intact, into 1cm cubes or so.

4. Throw the cubes into the pan with the salt, adding more water until it reaches slightly below the tops of the potato.

5. Roughly chop coconut block and add to simmering pot, along with passata.

6. Chop greens; and after about 5 minutes of simmering, add them to the pot.

7. Give ingredients a stir and cook for about 10 minutes further. Towards end of the cooking time, stir to encourage the sweet potato to fall apart. This stage will depend on how large you've chopped your sweet potatoes and the variety you've chosen.

Alternatives:

This soup can be varied by adding extra veggies. However, there are a few magical ingredients, as listed above, that make it special. If you don't have creamed coconut block then use 250ml of coconut cream from a tin or carton in place of the coconut block, using only 650ml of water.

Serenity Mint Pea Soup

Sometimes it's the simple, effortless blends that are the most rewarding.
This is a well loved favourite with our friends.

Serves: 4
Preparation time: 5 minutes
Cooking time: 15 minutes

Ingredients:

1 large potato
900g fresh or frozen garden peas
50g creamed coconut block
Large handful of fresh garden mint
(or 1 heaped tablespoon of dried spearmint)
1 teaspoon sea salt
700ml spring water

1. Chop potato (leave skin on) into small chunks.

2. Boil potato with salt, in a large cooking pot. Use enough water to just cover their tops, boiling until soft enough to pierce with a fork. This should take no more than 10 minutes.

3. Add frozen peas and bring back to the boil, adding the rest of the water.

4. Roughly chop coconut block and add to the peas, whilst the pot comes back to the boil.

5. Add mint.

6. Simmer for a few minutes once it has come back to the boil.

7. Blend thoroughly with a hand blender directly in the pan until nice and creamy, adding more water if the mixture is too thick for you.

Variation:

Use a 400ml tin of good quality, organic, coconut milk instead of coconut block and omit 500ml of water from the original ingredient list. Create as above.

Cosmic Coconut & Pumpkin Soup

This is one of those satiating, delicious creations that makes you feel incredibly loved up on a cold autumn evening. It's an excellent use for seasonal produce when the nights start getting darker. I say 'pumpkin', but the recipe is totally interchangeable with squash - in fact I frequently use butternut squash in place of pumpkin, for this recipe.

Serves: 4 hearty bowls
Preparation time: 15 minutes
Cooking time: 30 minutes

Ingredients:

2 medium sized leeks (finely chopped)
1 clove garlic (pressed or finely chopped)
1 large squash (or pumpkin) approx 1kg
1 heaped teaspoon ground cumin
2 heaped teaspoons ground coriander seed
200g block of coconut
1 small chopped bunch of fresh coriander
1 teaspoon sea salt
Filtered or spring water
A sprinkle of Love

1. Chop leek, crush garlic and sauté gently in a large pot for a couple of minutes.

2. Add the pumpkin along with enough water to reach just below the top of the contents in the cooking pot.

3. Bring to the boil, and then turn down to simmer gently for about 20 minutes.

4. Whilst simmering, add the ground coriander, ground cumin and salt.

5. Roughly chop the coconut block and add to pot whilst the soup is still simmering.

6. Roughly chop the fresh coriander and add to the pot a couple of minutes before the end of cooking time.

7. Allow the delightful aroma to flood your home.

8. Add a sprinkle of LOVE (for extra flavour!).

9. Blend altogether to make a thick creamy soup (if you don't have a blender you can use a potato masher, to roughly press through the soup, allowing the squash to thicken the preparation).

10. Enjoy!

Notes:

If you already have the oven on beforehand consider baking your pumpkin ahead of time. This can really bring out the flavour. Simply slice, de-seed, pop on a baking tray and bake until you can easily pierce a fork into it. Scoop the pumpkin away from the skin once cooled. Baking will effortlessly bring out the flavour. Make soup as described, reducing the cooking time.
Replace the coconut block with coconut cream from a carton or tin. Add 350ml of coconut cream with the initial water, allowing all liquid (water & cream) to come to just below top of contents .

"Cowardice asks the question: is it safe?
Expediency asks the question: is it politic?
Vanity asks the question: is it popular?
But conscience asks the question: is it right?
And there comes a time when one must take
a position that is neither safe, nor politic,
nor popular - but one must take it
simply because it is right."

~Martin Luther King, Jr.~

CREAMY CAULIFLOWER & COCONUT SOUP

The dance of nutmeg and coconut in this soup will send forth an exotic aroma, to flood your senses with a 'little bit of divine'. It is delicious. Both cauliflower and nutmeg are full of health giving properties, which enliven me every time I eat this.

Serves: 4
Preparation time: 15 minutes
Cooking time: 20 minutes

Ingredients:

1 large cauliflower
1 medium sweet potato
1 large onion
1 tablespoon olive oil
200g creamed coconut block
1 teaspoon freshly ground nutmeg
1 handful of chopped garden herbs
 (e.g. rosemary, thyme, parsley, sage)
1 teaspoon sea salt (or to taste)
Water (approx 600ml)

1. Chop the cauliflower into pieces and the sweet potatoes into half inch cubes.

2. Finely chop the onion.

3. Heat the oil in a large cooking pan.

4. Gently sauté the onion for a couple of minutes before adding the cauliflower. Stir often over a period of a few minutes.

5. Add the sweet potatoes.

6. Add the water to reach a couple of centimeters below the top of the ingredients (approximately 600ml).

7. Toss in the sea salt and herbs (saving a bit of parsley to garnish) whilst bringing contents to the boil.

8. Roughly chop the coconut and add to the pan.

9. Once boiling, reduce the heat to a simmer and allow it to cook for 20 minutes. Grate the nutmeg and add during the cooking period, enjoying the delightful aroma.

10. Once cooked it is ready to blend. Give it a few pulses to make it thick and creamy.

11. Finely chop the remaining parsley and use it to garnish each bowl of soup as you serve (nothing like a bit of garnish to make it feel posh!).

Variation:
If you don't have creamed coconut block, then substitute for coconut cream from a carton or tin. Use 350ml of coconut cream and adjust the water quantity to 200ml.
Replacing the sweet potato with regular potato works well.

BARLEY STEW

This is one of those deep winter, comforting meals, that will leave you feeling brimming. Sometimes it's the only thing that will do. It fills you up, yet digests easily and gives an excellent top up of B vitamins in the process.

Tip: Plan ahead and leave the barley and split peas to soak in the water for a few hours to speed up cooking time.

Cooking time can vary between batches of barley. Count on up to an hour.

Makes: 4 bowlfuls
Cooking time: Up to 1 hour

Ingredients:

200g flavoursome mushrooms
1 large onion
250g pearl barley
150g green split peas
1.5 litres spring or filtered water
1 medium sized swede
  (or 1 small/medium sweet potato)
Nettles (a big loose salad bowl full)
  (or kale - several large leaves)
Fresh herbs: rosemary, parsley
  (a good handful of both mixed together)
Thyme (a heaped teaspoons worth)
1 teaspoon sea salt (or to taste)
1 tin (400g) chopped tomatoes
  (or even better - 8 fresh tomatoes)

1. Roughly chop the onion and mushrooms and then gently sauté in a large cooking pot.

2. Add the barley, split peas, water and salt to the pot.

3. Bring to the boil, whilst finely chopping and adding the herbs.

4. In the meantime, chop the swede (including skin) into small squares no larger than 1cm cubed.

5. After the pot has been simmering for 20 minutes add the swede and tin of tomatoes.

6. Allow to cook until all the water has absorbed and the barley and split peas have softened. This may take between 45 minutes and one hour if you haven't pre-soaked the barley and split peas; less time if they have been soaked already.

Notes:

If you can't get swede, use sweet potato.
Dried parsley is fine instead of fresh (but use less).
If nettles are in season, then I highly recommend them – if not available, then use kale.

CARROT & CORIANDER SOUP

Good old carrot and coriander!
Add lentils and a few extras and you've got a well rounded, satiating meal in a pot.

Serves: 3
Preparation & cooking: 35 minutes

Ingredients:

50g red lentils
400ml water
500g carrots
1 medium onion
1 large garlic clove
1 small courgette
2 heaped teaspoons ground coriander
1 teaspoon ground cumin
200g passatta (unsalted)
½ teaspoon sea salt
Pinch black pepper
Handful fresh coriander

1. Add water and lentils to a medium sized pan and bring to the boil.

2. Chop carrot and courgette into small pieces.

3. Roughly chop onion and crush (or finely chop) garlic.

4. Add all ingredients (except fresh coriander) to the pan once the lentils have been cooking for a few minutes.

5. Bring back to the boil and cook gently for 20 minutes.

6. Remove pan from the heat and add handful of roughly chopped fresh coriander. You don't have to blend this although it does help the flavours to dance together. Use a hand blender to pulsate soup a few times to get the rustic effect with lots of vibrant speckles throughout.

7. This also serves really well if you cook it in advance and then heat it up later.

Tomato Lovers Soup

This is the easiest soup ever! Beats the shop bought tinned varieties any day, with the added bonus that you can whip it up very fast. This makes a great base with which to add other ingredients, such as chickpeas, beans, broccoli, cabbage or kale.

Makes: 2 - 3 bowls
Cooking time: 5 minutes

Ingredients:

50g creamed coconut block
700g unsalted passata (approx)
1 teaspoon sea salt
1 heaped teaspoon of cornflour
100ml water to thin down
Handful of basil (optional)

1. Roughly chop the coconut block.

2. Mix the cornflour thoroughly with the cold water, making sure that there are no lumps.

3. Throw all the ingredients together in a pan (apart from the basil).

4. Cook on the stove until the coconut has melted (approximately 5 minutes) adding the freshly chopped or torn basil in the final minute or two.

Variations:

Add chickpeas, butter beans or pre-cooked veggies in at the start.
Add a couple of cloves of garlic and a handful of parsley.
Use 125ml of coconut cream in place of the coconut block, but omit the 100ml of water.

SPLIT PEA SOUP

Split pea soup has an interesting earthy quality. The high protein content of the split peas and the subtle combination of flavours make for a lovely grounding soup. You can use either green or yellow split peas.

Serves: 2
Preparation: 5 minutes
Cooking: 40 minutes

Ingredients:

200g split peas
600ml water
3 whole bay leaves
2 large garlic cloves
½ teaspoon sea salt
Twist black pepper
200g tinned tomatoes
A loose handful parsley

1. Put dried split peas into a pan with 600ml of water and bring to the boil.

2. In the meantime, add the whole bay leaves to the simmering pot. **A word of caution**: bay leaves are just for flavour. You will be removing them near the end of the recipe, so keep them whole, otherwise you'll have a right job on your hands fishing out the bits!

3. Crush and add the garlic to pan, along with salt and pepper.

4. Once the pot is boiling, turn heat down to low, allow the water to simmer for approximately 35 minutes or until split peas have softened. Keep an eye on the water, in case it boils dry or bubbles over. If necessary add a little more water.

5. Finely chop the parsley.

6. After about 20 minutes mix in the tomatoes and parsley (saving a little bit of parsley to garnish).

7. **Important:** take out and compost the bay leaves at the end of cooking period.

8. Use a hand blender to pulsate and blend the ingredients together.

"A human being is a part of the whole
called by us universe,
a part limited in time and space.
He experiences himself, his thoughts and feeling
as something separated from the rest,
a kind of optical delusion of his consciousness.
This delusion is a kind of prison for us,
restricting us to our personal desires and to
affection for a few persons nearest to us.
Our task must be to free ourselves from this prison
by widening our circle of compassion
to embrace all living creatures and
the whole of nature in its beauty."

~Albert Einstein~

Main dishes

The dishes in this section were created especially to help build a bridge to a more healthy way of eating. They are delicious, nutritious and full of high quality vibrational goodness. These meals frequently make an appearance during the spiritual retreats and courses that I facilitate with my husband. I've included some classic 'feel good' food dishes that give a satiated kind of feeling. Enjoy with salad or lightly steamed vegetables.

Conscious Cottage Pie

A delicious and well loved, conscious alternative to the traditional meaty variety.

Serves: 6
Preparation: 30 minutes
Cooking: 75 – 90 minutes

Ingredients:

Main ingredients:
1 medium sized leek
1 large clove garlic
1 large bell pepper (optional)
Two handfuls mushrooms
250g puy lentils
600ml water
1 vegan stock cube
400g tin chopped tomatoes
  (or unsalted passata)
½ teaspoon sea salt
2 teaspoons ground cinnamon
1 teaspoon allspice
1 teaspoon (heaped) onion
  granules
2 tablespoons date syrup
1 handful chopped fresh parsley
  (or 1 tablespoon dried)
1 to 2 tablespoons olive oil

Topping ingredients:
750g potatoes (not peeled)
50g creamed coconut block
100ml rice milk
Sprinkle of salt
Sprinkle dried parsley

How to prepare main ingredients:
1. Chop leek and finely chop or crush the garlic.
2. Chop the pepper and mushrooms.
3. Heat olive oil in a pan on medium heat.
4. Gently sauté the leek and garlic for two minutes.
5. Add the pepper and mushrooms and sauté for a couple of minutes (adding a little extra oil if needed).
6. Add the puy lentils along with the water, stock cube and tin of tomatoes and then bring to the boil.
7. Add the salt, herbs, spices and remaining ingredients, then allow to simmer for about 45 minutes, stirring frequently. All of the water should be absorbed (if it isn't then give it more time to cook). The puy lentils should hold their shape, yet have a soft bite.

Topping - mashed potatoes:
1. Whilst the main pot is simmering, chop and cook the unpeeled potatoes.
2. Finely chop the creamed coconut block with a sharp knife.
3. Chop the unpeeled potatoes into pieces (the smaller they are the faster they will cook).
4. Once cooked, drain off the water and sprinkle in the coconut, giving it a quick mix to distribute the coconut a little into the potato. Replace the lid and allow the coconut to melt for a few minutes. Then add the salt and rice milk.
5. Mash with a potato masher until it is lump free, achieving a creamy consistency.

Bringing it all together:
1. When lentil mixture is cooked, pour into a casserole dish.
2. Spoon the potato evenly on top, covering the lentil mixture entirely.
3. Use a fork to spread out the potato, creating 'ridges' on the top.
4. Lovingly sprinkle a small amount of dried parsley on top.
5. Bake in a hot oven for about 25 minutes or long enough to allow the topping to crisp. Temperature gas mark 6 (200°C/400°F).

BENEVOLENT BAKE

This is a satisfying vegetable crumble designed to be interchangeable with whatever veggies are in season.

Serves: 4
Preparation: 30 minutes
Cooking time: 30 minutes

Ingredients:

Topping ingredients:

50g shelled sunflower seeds
150g oatmeal (or rolled oats)
1 tablespoon fresh rosemary
Pinch of sea salt
5 tablespoons olive oil
2 tablespoons water

Filling ingredients:

1 large head of broccoli
½ tin of butter beans (optional)
Handful of green beans
or mangetout
1 small leek
Handful of tasty mushrooms
1 small courgette
1 large handful of fresh spinach
or nettles

Sauce ingredients:

2 heaped teaspoons cornflour
300ml water
1 tablespoon (15ml) tamari
100g creamed coconut block
or alternatively
use mushroom gravy as sauce
instead (see page 129)

How to prepare:

Topping:

1. Roughly grind seeds in a nut mill.

2. De-stalk and finely chop rosemary.

3. Mix seeds, oatmeal, herbs and sea salt together in a mixing bowl.

4. Make a well in the middle and then add the oil.

5. Mix together with a spoon until the topping is moist, yet still crumbly. You might like to start using your hands once the oil has been mixed in. If a little more moisture is needed then add a small amount of extra oil, a teaspoon at a time.

6. Put your topping to the side while you prepare the filling and sauce.

Filling:

1. Chop broccoli (including stalk - except for the tough bits) and all other filling ingredients.

2. Steam broccoli, leek and green beans for 7 minutes. Toss in the mushrooms, courgette and leaves right at the end of the steaming period (these unsteamed veggies will bake in the oven instead).

3. Make the sauce whilst steaming the above.

Sauce:

Make the sauce whilst the vegetables are steaming.

1. Mix the cornflour with water in a sauce pan, adding the tamari.

2. Gently heat up, stirring frequently. The sauce will suddenly begin to thicken as it reaches boiling point. At this stage, stir continuously to avoid lumps forming.

3. Roughly chop the coconut block and stir until it has thoroughly melted in. You should have a thick creamy sauce.

Bringing the bake together:

Mix sauce and steamed veggies together in a baking dish (approximately 25cm x 20cm).

Evenly add topping and gently press down by hand.

Place in a preheated oven at gas mark 6 (200°C/400°F) for about 30 minutes (or until the topping begins to tan).

Alternatives:

If you don't have ground sunflower seeds then try replacing with more oatmeal, regular rolled oats or spelt flour. Alternatively, roughly grinding your seeds with a pestle and mortar works fine too, because you are aiming for a crumble, rather than a pastry.

Try making the topping exclusively with spelt flour as a variation.

Cut down on effort and washing up by skipping the steaming process. Simply make as above, mixing your raw veggies with the sauce, but bake for 40 minutes instead. Works just as well.

CAMPFIRE BEANS

This recipe came into being a few years ago. My dearest friend Stephi and I were preparing food for an intensive week-long spiritual course in the foothills of Mount Snowdon in Wales. Intense work often calls for grounding foods. We'd put the baked potatoes into the open fire as the recipe for homemade baked beans danced and wove itself into being. This is a super healthy, flavoursome alternative to one of Britain's all time favourite supermarket foods. Campfire beans (which really don't need to be cooked on a campfire) go perfectly with baked potatoes and salad. They freeze well and mature wonderfully when reheated.

Serves: 8
Preparation: 15 minutes
Cooking time: 30 minutes

Ingredients:

4 to 5 tins of haricot beans
 (or equivalent amount from hard haricot beans - approx 500g soaked overnight and boiled until soft yields about 1kg)
1 bottle of salt free passata
 (approx 690g)
2 tablespoons date syrup
 (or apple juice concentrate)
3 tablespoons apple cider vinegar
3 tablespoons tamari or shoyu
1 medium or large onion
2 cloves garlic
2 heaped teaspoons gr. cinnamon
2 heaped teaspoons dried parsley
 (or one handful of fresh)
1 heaped teaspoon ground coriander
1 tablespoon olive oil

1. Finely chop onion and crush garlic.

2. Gently sauté garlic and onion in bottom of a large pan for a couple of minutes with the olive oil.

3. Add all other ingredients to the pan and stir thoroughly together.

4. Gently bring back to the boil and then simmer for up to half an hour to allow the flavours to dance together. If you are serving it later, then simmer it for ten minutes, stirring occasionally and leave to stew in its own warmth. Stir in thoroughly and reheat before serving. If you are however, serving it there and then, allow it to simmer for half and hour to let the flavours infuse, with occasional stirring.

Variations:
Use fresh, baked tomatoes or tinned tomatoes instead of passata, but blend to form a thick liquid first. Add a hint of chilli if you like it hot.

SEED LOAF

On Christmas day a few years back, we all wanted some kind of 'nut roast' type thing to enjoy with vegetables, roast potatoes and gravy. I rose to the challenge, feeling inspired to use sunflower seeds, rather than nuts. We were thrilled with the appetizing result. This seed roast is surprisingly light and easy to digest. It serves delightfully with mushroom gravy (see pg 129).

Serves: 4
Preparation: 25 minutes
Cooking time: 45 minutes

Ingredients:

*Carrots 4 – 5 medium sized
(or 400g approx)*
150g ground sunflower seeds
150g ground pumpkin seeds
2 cloves garlic
1 heaped tablespoon rosemary
*1 heaped tablespoon fresh parsley
(or 1 heaped teaspoon dried)*
1 teaspoon sea salt

1. Chop the (unpeeled, but scrubbed) carrots into small pieces. Boil or steam until soft. Drain and then mash.

2. Grind seeds in a nut mill to make seed meal.

3. Crush garlic and finely chop rosemary and parsley.

4. Mix seed meal, carrots and all other ingredients together.

5. Firmly press mixture into a loaf tin (lined with parchment paper). A 1kg loaf tin works well (approx 20x10x-6cm). Make sure that you press really firmly to encourage the binding process - if you are too timid, it tends to fall apart. If you get it just right, then it magically forms into a perfectly sliceable loaf.

6. Bake in a preheated oven at gas mark 6 (200°C/400°F) for approximately 45 minutes.

7. Gently lift from the loaf tin by pulling out the loaf along with the parchment paper. Turn over onto a bread board and slice with a bread knife.

Notes:

Grinding the seeds works best with a seed/nut/coffee grinder, although you can use a blender to roughly chop the seeds instead. If you roughly chop the seeds, then add a heaped tablespoon of spelt flour to the mixture to encourage the binding process. The other alternative is to use a pestle and mortar.

If you have neither a grinder nor a blender, you can substitute the ground seeds for pre-ground nuts or seeds.

SUNSET SWEET POTATOES (MILD CURRY)

This is an exquisite, exotic medley, that can be served as a curry on rice.
We also enjoy it as a side accompaniment to a salad.

Serves: 4
Preparation: 10 minutes
Cooking: 30 - 40 minutes

Ingredients:

350ml to 500ml spring water (see notes *)
150g coconut block
3 medium/large sweet potatoes
 (approx 1 to 1.25kg in weight)
1 clove garlic
200g chickpeas (drained & pre-cooked)
400g passata (or tin of chopped tomatoes)
1 level tablespoon medium curry powder
1 teaspoon sea salt
Pinch of ground cardamom
1 very large handful fresh coriander
1 handful fresh basil
200g organic sweetcorn kernels

1. Place water in large cooking pot and bring to the boil.

2. In the meantime, roughly chop coconut block, place in pot and allow to melt into the water to form 'coconut milk'.

3. Chop the sweet potato into roughly 2cm squares and crush the garlic.

4. Add chickpeas, sweet potatoes, garlic, tomatoes, curry powder, sea salt and half of the coriander (roughly chopped) to the coconut milk.

5. Bring to the boil and then allow to simmer on a low heat for approximately 35 minutes, stirring occasionally.

6. Toward the latter part of the cooking period the potatoes should begin to fall apart helping the sauce to thicken (cook a little longer if the sweet potatoes are still firm). Add sweetcorn and then at this final stage, roughly chop the basil and remaining coriander, then add to the pot.

Notes and variations:

* If you are cooking to serve immediately, use less water. The sauce should thicken nicely when the sweet potato begins to fall apart. It thickens even more if you leave it for a few hours. You can always add more water later if required.*

Try replacing half of the sweet potatoes with regular potatoes.

If you don't have creamed coconut block try using coconut cream from a tin or carton. Add 250ml of coconut cream and create as above changing the water quantity to 200ml.

Add copious amounts of fresh nettle leaves for a high energy extravaganza!

"Should you really open your eyes and see,
you would behold your image in all images.
And should you open your ears and listen,
you would hear your own voice in all voices."

~Kahlil Gibran~

BAKED FALAFEL

This is a middle eastern dish. It is traditionally deep fried, yet we can enjoy a more healthy version by baking it in an oven. Falafel serves well with hummus and pita bread. Here's the conscious kitchen version.

Makes: 12 balls
Preparation: 15 minutes
Cooking: 30 minutes

Ingredients:

500g chickpeas (or 2 tins drained)
2 large cloves garlic
1 tablespoon heaped fresh parsley
2 teaspoons heaped ground coriander
1 teaspoon heaped ground cumin
2 tablespoons olive oil
1½ teaspoons sea salt
2 tablespoons water (optional)
2 tablespoons spelt flour (optional)

1. Crush garlic and roughly chop parsley.
2. Add all ingredients into blender or food processor. This works best in two lots. Blend until most of the mixture is broken down. It doesn't need to be totally smooth; it can be quite rustic.
3. Place everything in a large mixing bowl. Mix everything together thoroughly again (with a spoon rather than a blender at this stage).
4. Mixture should 'hold together'. If it's starting to bind when you press with the back of your spoon it's probably fine. Try rolling a golf ball sized shape in your hands. If it doesn't hold then add a little water (a LITTLE at a time - you don't want to over-do it)… until desired consistency is achieved. Add a little spelt flour if needed. Chickpea moisture varies from batch to batch, affecting the bind-ability.
5. Place on a lightly oiled baking tray and bake in pre-heated oven at gas mark 6 or 7 (200°C to 220°C) for approximately 30 minutes or until tanned.

Veggie Stir-Steam

I love this alternative to the traditional stir fry. It's much more steamed than fried. The veggies are meant to have a wholesome 'al dente' bite, preserving more of their goodness. If you'd prefer them to be softer, just cook it a little longer. We eat this with organic wheat-free pasta or rice.

Serves: 2 - 3
Preparation: 20 minutes
Cooking: 7 minutes

Ingredients:

Main ingredients:
1 large onion
2 handfuls of mushrooms
½ medium broccoli head
1 courgette
A handful of mangetout
2 large carrots
A dash of coconut oil
3 tablespoons of water (approx)

Sauce ingredients:
1 inch cubed ginger
1 tablespoon tamari
1 tablespoon apple juice concentrate
2 tablespoons apple cider vinegar
1 heaped teaspoon cornflour
2 tablespoons water
Pinch of black pepper

1. Peel and finely grate the ginger.
2. Mix all of the sauce ingredients together. The important thing is that the cornflour dissolves completely. Put sauce to the side until the end of the cooking period.
3. Thinly slice the carrots and chop the broccoli into small florets. Chop the rest of the vegetables how ever you like.
4. Using a medium sized cooking pot, melt a little coconut oil. Toss in the onion and mushrooms and fry in the oil for 1 - 2 minutes whilst stirring frequently.
5. Put rest of the vegetables into the pan adding about 3 tablespoons of water. The water should come to the boil very quickly on a high heat. Stir in the vegetables and allow the steam from the small amount of water to steam the contents of the pot. Stir frequently, replacing the lid after each stir over a period of approximately 5 minutes.
6. Near the end of the cooking period give the sauce a quick stir and then pour into the hot pan. Stir all contents with sauce continuously for about a minute. Once the cornflour hits the heat, it will rapidly turn into a thick sauce to coat the veggies.
7. Serve with wheat-free pasta, rice or quinoa.

STUFFED SUMMER PEPPERS

The brilliant thing about this dish is that it can be served both raw or baked.
They are tasty and wholesome and serve wonderfully with salad and rice.

Preparation: 20 minutes
Cooking: 15 - 20 minutes
Serves: 3

Ingredients:
3 sweet peppers
150g sunflower seeds
2 medium sized carrots
1 clove garlic
1 tablespoon chopped parsley
1 tablespoon chopped rosemary
3 tablespoons sunflower oil
1 tablespoon tamari
  (or sea salt to taste)

1. Cut bell peppers in half, scooping out the seeds and whites to make two boats with each pepper.

2. Grind seeds in a nut mill, coffee grinder or with a pestle and mortar.

3. Grate carrots.

4. Crush garlic.

5. Finely chop rosemary and parsley.

6. Mix all ingredients (apart from the pepper) in a large bowl until thoroughly combined. The consistency will be similar to a loose pâté.

7. Share mixture evenly between the pepper boats, compressing downwards as you stuff them.

8. Bake in a preheated oven at gas mark 7 (425°F / 220°C) for about 15 - 20 minutes (or until they begin to tan/gently crisp on top).

Quinoa Medley

This has to be my favourite cooked dish. It's a colourful medley of delicious, super health affirming foods. This welcoming array of whole and complete nutrients make it a perfect main meal, although it works equally well as a side dish. The quinoa is cooked, making it easier to digest, whilst all other ingredients are gently tossed in at the end, keeping their optimal nutritional value.

Serves: 1
Preparation: 10 minutes
Cooking: 15 minutes

Ingredients:

100g quinoa
350ml water
1 tablespoon tamari
1 large garlic clove
1 small handful cherry tomatoes
1 loose handful fresh parsley
1 small ripe avocado
1 tablespoon hemp oil

1. Boil quinoa in a cooking pot with water, until all of the water has been absorbed. This should take up to 15 minutes. Keep a close eye on it after about 10 minutes to avoid it burning.

2. Whilst the quinoa is cooking prepare the rest of the ingredients.

3. Crush garlic.

4. Quarter your cherry tomatoes.

5. Dice avocado.

6. Destalk and roughly tear parsley.

7. When the quinoa has absorbed all of the water, take it off the heat and stir in the tamari.

8. Toss in the remaining ingredients before stirring in the hemp oil.

9. Enjoy whilst it is still warm, with salad leaves on the side.

QUINOA (pronounced "keen-wa")

Thought to have originated from South America, this incredible 'nutty' food has been harvested for its edible, grain-like seeds for thousands of years. We now have at least a couple of varieties that have succeeded in Europe. I am very keen to see this grown locally, wherever possible, so that we can rely much less on imports that potentially denature local economies abroad.

Quinoa can be used in place of rice or other grains. It also works well raw and sprouted (see *page 57* for quinoa sprouting guidance).

Quinoa is an excellent source of protein, vitamin A, manganese, phosphorus, folic acid, potassium and magnesium. It boasts an impressive array of amino acids (essential for tissue repair and growth).

There is a related species called "fat hen" or "goosefoot" (*Chenopodium album*) commonly found as a 'weed' in the summer throughout temperate regions. An excellent leafy vegetable to delight any forager. The green leaves can be eaten as you would spinach, although best in moderation due to high levels of oxalic acid. The seeds can also be used as a grain, just like quinoa.

Our side dishes and extras work well to give a boost to the salads and main meals, should you need a little something more.

Sides & Extras

TURMERIC RICE

Turmeric has such a catalogue of health benefits, that I just had to include one of our regular turmeric rice dishes in this section. There's a bit of a knack to cooking rice. Different types of rice require different amounts of water and different cooking times. This recipe is for long grain rice, but if like me, you like to use whatever is available, then please do go ahead and substitute for an alternative type of rice. Adjust water quantities and cooking times accordingly. If in doubt use less water than listed here, keep an eye on the pan and add more if you need it.

Serves: 2
Preparation: 5 minutes
Cooking: 50 minutes

Ingredients:
175g brown long grain rice
100g mushrooms
1 large garlic clove
Dash of olive oil
700 ml water
½ teaspoon sea salt
1 level teaspoon ground turmeric
Pinch of ground cardamom
A few parsley sprigs

1. Crush garlic and chop mushrooms, then gently sauté for a couple of minutes in a medium sized pan.
2. Add rice, water and all remaining ingredients, except parsley.
3. Bring to the boil and cook on a medium heat, with a loose lid on the pan, for about 35-40 minutes, stirring occasionally.
4. All of the water should have been absorbed at this point. Turn off the heat. Mix in the chopped parsley and secure the lid. If the lid isn't exactly tight fitting, then place a couple of thick hand towels over the top to keep the heat in. Leave to steam in its own heat (without the stove heating element) for about 10 minutes.
5. After 10 minutes remove lid, stir and serve.

ROAST VEGGIES

I must admit, I am a bit of a raw or steamed veg fan myself. I nearly always go for that pure, minimalist vibe. However, roast veggies are still like a real treat, not to be missed. They're perfect for entertaining guests. You can chop well in advance and whip them out to pop in the oven once the clock starts ticking; they'll work their own culinary magic with very little attention, leaving you to lovingly weave the rest of dinner. The ingredients are interchangeable. These are just suggestions.

Serves: 4
Preparation: 10 minutes
Cooking: 35 - 45 minutes

Ingredients:
½ small swede
½ butternut squash
2 courgettes
3 small red onions
3 parsnips
2 cloves garlic
Handful rosemary
Sprig of thyme
Sea salt
Drizzle of olive oil

1. Preheat oven to gas mark 7 (220°C/425°F).
2. Cut onions into wedges and crush garlic.
3. Slice parsnips, swede and courgette into wedges.
4. Scoop out seeds from squash. Peel the skin and chop squash into wedges.
5. Lay out all mixed veggies into one or two oven trays.
6. Roughly chop rosemary and pick off thyme leaves before sprinkling over the veg.
7. Drizzle a little olive oil over the veggies and pop into the oven.
8. Shake the oven tray a few times during the cooking period to evenly cook the veggies.

HEMPY NETTLED POTATOES

This is an awesome way to enjoy potatoes with an added touch of two of my favourite high vibrational superfoods - nettles and hemp oil.

This works a treat alongside salads.

Serves: 2
Preparation: 10 minutes
Cooking: 10 minutes

Ingredients:

400g potato
100ml - 200ml spring water
50g nettle leaves
Dash of hemp oil
Dash of tamari

1. Chop the potato into small cubes (roughly 1.5cm cubed).

2. Add potatoes into a cooking pan along with the water. The amount of water you need will vary depending on your cooker and the potatoes that you use. Start with 100ml and add more as required.

3. Bring to the boil and allow to simmer gently, stirring occasionally, over about ten minutes (or until you can easily push a fork through them). Keep an eye on the pan in case it starts to boil dry. Whilst they are cooking, destalk and chop nettles.

4. By the time they are cooked there should be very little water left in.

5. Toss in the nettles and cook for a further minute or two, to denature the nettle sting.

6. If there is any water left in the pan, drain it off.

7. Pop it on your plate ready to serve, drizzling a splash of hemp oil and tamari over the top to taste (you can also do this in the pan before serving, but I feel that it is a bit of a shame to waste the good oil that ends up sticking to the sides of your cooking pot).

Alternatives:

If you are avoiding potatoes (which I often do), then try this with sweet potatoes or swede for a delicious alternative.

STINGING NETTLES – Natures superfood

A gift of nirvanic heaven if there ever was one. The faithful nettle is one of my top five foods of all time. It is found all over the world, although it seems to thrive in temperate zones.

The best time to pick nettles is before they start developing seeds. The seed produces an irritant that may bother some folk. Spring is normally the best time to pick, although if you cut them right back after the first seeding, you will get new growth later in the season too. The youngest, freshest leaves, without the stalks, are optimal.

Nettles can also be dehydrated, stored and then crumbled to sprinkle on salads or brewed as tea for use all year round.

Unless you are feeling brave, I recommend gathering stinging nettles with rubber gloves. Drying or soaking in water or sauce/oil will instantly remove the sting, making them edible both raw and cooked.

Nettles have been shown to aid and cure a myriad of health conditions since ancient times. Nutritionally, they have high levels of iron, sulphur, calcium, potassium and silica, as well as other trace minerals. They are rich in vitamins A, B, C, D, and K and said to be one of the most substantial sources of chlorophyll in the vegetable world.

Some other recipes with nettles:

Sundried tomato and nettle pâté... *page 67*
Barley stew... *page 90*
Trin's soul food special... *page 83*
Nettle and mushroom stir fry... *page 125*

PEASE PUDDING

Pease pudding is a traditional, North-East England dish that I enjoyed whilst growing up. Owing to the favourable response of everyone who seems to eat it, pease pudding has well and truly earned its place here. Eat with potatoes, veggies, barley, rice, salad, put it in a sandwich or use it cold as a dip. This multi-talented, protein packed dish just works! Here's the conscious kitchen version.

Serves: 2
Preparation: 5 minutes
Cooking: 40 minutes

Ingredients:

200g split peas
450ml to 500ml water
3 whole bay leaves
1 large clove garlic
½ teaspoon sea salt
Twist black pepper
200g tinned tomatoes

1. Put dried split peas in a pan with 450ml of water and bring to the boil.
2. In the meantime, add the whole bay leaves to the simmering pot. **A word of caution**: bay leaves are just for flavour. You will be removing them near the end of the recipe, so keep them whole.
3. Crush and add the garlic to pan, along with salt and pepper.
4. Once the pot is boiling, turn heat down to low, allow the water to simmer for approximately 35 minutes or until split peas have softened. Keep an eye on the water in case it boils dry or bubbles over. If necessary add a little more water.
5. After about 20 minutes, mix in the tomatoes.
6. **Important:** when all water has been absorbed, take out and compost the bay leaves.
7. Use a hand blender to pulsate and blend the ingredients together until you achieve a thick pâté consistency.
8. Serve immediately with dinner or allow it to cool and use as a pâté with salad or in a salad sandwich. It keeps well in a container in the fridge for about a week and a half.

Chunky Wedges

Everybody seems to loves the humble potato, so these are a bit of an all round winner that serves well with just about anything. You can also create a lovely side dish by doing the same with sweet potato and parsnips.

Preparation: 5 minutes
Cooking: 35 - 45 minutes

Ingredients:

One large potato per person
Dash of olive oil
Sprinkle of sea salt
Sprinkle of finely chopped herbs
i.e. rosemary, oregano, thyme

1. Preheat oven to gas mark 6 (200˚C / 400˚F).
2. Finely chop herbs (or used dried, mixed, crushed herbs instead).
3. Chop potato into wedges and evenly spread on a baking tray.
4. Splash a dash of oil onto potatoes along with herbs and salt. Swish them around to coat ingredients evenly.
5. Bake for about 30 minutes or until they are golden. You can tell if they are ready when you can put a fork through them without resistance.

Quinoa Sweetcorn

Not only is this dish tasty and wonderfully delicious, it is really fast to make. Throw some salad greens or veggies on the side and you have a filling meal fit for a quinoa king and queen!

Serves: 2
Preparation: 2 minutes
Cooking: 15 minutes

Ingredients:

200g quinoa
600-700ml water
100g tinned sweetcorn
1 tablespoon tamari (or to taste)
2 tablespoons hemp oil

This recipe is designed to soak up all the water on cooking, although if there is a little left over at the end of the cooking period, just strain it off before adding the tamari and hemp oil.

1. Bring quinoa to the boil with the water in a medium sized pan and cook for approximately 15 minutes, until the quinoa is soft and has absorbed the water.
2. Drain the sweetcorn and add into the pan a few minutes before the end of the cooking period.
3. Strain water off if there is any excess.
4. Stir in tamari and hemp oil and serve immediately.

Mushroom Millet

Millet is a nutritional, gluten free, grain-like seed. It's well worth adding to your diet, although it helps to know what to do with it. Most people find it a little bland without a little jazzing up. It's quick to cook and dances well with a few little extras thrown in.
Here's how we like it...

Serves: 2
Preparation: 5 minutes
Cooking: 12 minutes

Ingredients:

200g millet
450ml water
100g mushrooms
1 small red onion
1 heaped teaspoon dried parsley
(or 1 tablespoon fresh)
1 to 2 tablespoons olive oil
1 tablespoon shoyu
1 tablespoon hemp oil (optional)

1. Chop onion and mushrooms, then gently sauté for a couple of minutes in a pot, using the olive oil.

2. Once onion and mushrooms have been sautéed, add the millet, water and parsley to the pot. Bring to the boil and cook on a medium heat for approximately 10 minutes or until all of the water has been absorbed into the millet. The millet should be soft, yet still retaining it's shape.

3. When the cooking has finished, mix in the shoyu and serve.

4. Drizzle some hemp oil (or your favourite cold pressed oil) over the top before eating.

Variation:

Try "sweetcorn millet". Leave out the mushrooms, onion and parsley, adding a handful of fresh/frozen or tinned organic sweetcorn kernels into the pot instead.

Simple Baked Sweet Potatoes

You could make this into a fancy dish, with all sorts of toppings and things, but to be honest, there is absolutely nothing wrong with a good old fashioned simple, baked sweet potato. They serve beautifully loaded with homemade baked beans or with a sliver of melted coconut butter.

Preparation: 2 minutes
Cooking: 45 - 60 minutes

Ingredient:

Sweet potato

1. Scrub sweet potatoes and pierce with a fork.

2. Place on a baking tray and pop into an oven preheated to about gas mark 6 (200°C/400°F).

3. Bake for about 45 minutes (depending on the size of your potatoes), or until they are soft to pierce with a fork. They hit the sweet spot of perfection when they are soft, yet not oozing.

4. Serve right away or enjoy cold with salad later.

Grilled Garlic Mushrooms

Juicy, delicious mushrooms with a hint of garlic never go amiss.
To avoid confusion if you live in the US, be aware that my grilling is actually
the equivalent of your 'broiling'.

Serves: 2
Preparation: 5 minutes
Cooking: 5 minutes

Ingredients:

100g chestnut mushrooms
1 medium clove garlic
1 tablespoon olive oil
Pinch sea salt

1. Remove stalks from the mushrooms and place the mushrooms upside down, on a baking sheet or grill pan.

2. Crush garlic and then mix in a small bowl with olive oil and salt.

3. Share the oil mixture evenly between all of the upturned mushrooms.

4. Grill the upside down mushroom boats for up to five minutes under a medium heat. You can see that they are cooked when they start to look a bit shrivelled.

"There is a Light that shines beyond
all things on earth,
beyond us all,
beyond the heavens,
beyond the highest heavens.
This is the Light that shines in our hearts."
~Chandogya Upanishad~

Mushroom & Nettle Stir-Fry

There is something about this dish that leaves people feeling really good. This stir-fry offers an excellent portion of superfood that makes me savour every mouthful as a divine gift from Gaia.

Serves: 2
Preparation: 15 minutes
Cooking: 5 minutes

Ingredients:

250g tasty mushrooms
50g (minimum) nettles
2 tablespoons olive oil
1 tablespoon shoyu

1. Gather a large salad serving bowl full of loose, fresh nettles using gloves or something to protect your hands. Nettles are best eaten when they are young, before they've gone to seed (seeds are best avoided).

2. Chop mushrooms.

3. Destalk and roughly chop nettles (still using gloves).

4. Pour the olive oil into either a frying pan or a regular pan and turn on to a high-ish heat. Drop in the mushrooms, stirring regularly for about 3 minutes or until they seem to have cooked and heated through.

5. Then toss in the nettles, stirring a few times over a two minute period. Use a lid to keep the moisture in between stirs. Add the shoyu during this process. The nettle sting should disappear pretty rapidly upon contact with the hot steam from the cooking.

6. After a couple of minutes, stir one last time and take off the heat. Replace the lid and leave the flavours to permeate through each other for a few minutes until serving with the rest of your meal.

'Out There' Oatcakes

These savoury, crunchy biscuits go down really well with soup, or hummus and salad. Homemade oatcakes don't seem to last five minutes on our dining table.

Makes: about 20 oatcakes
Preparation time: 20 minutes
Cooking time: 20 - 25 minutes

Ingredients:

200g oatmeal
100g ground seed or nuts
 (i.e. sunflower/pumpkin/almond)
½ teaspoon sea salt (or to taste)
200ml approx filtered or spring water
50g spelt flour or fine oatmeal to roll with
A dash of oil for oven tray

Other things that you'll need:

Rolling pin
Cookie cutter or sharp knife
Oven tray

1. Turn oven on to approximately gas mark 7 (220°C / 425°F).

2. Mix all dry ingredients together.

3. Add 150ml of the water and mix thoroughly with the dry ingredients. Add the remaining 50ml of water a little at a time, until you have a dough-like 'rollable' ball (the best way to mix is to use the back of a spoon, with a pressing type motion). When you have added all water necessary, press firmly together with your hands. You may be tempted to add more water to get it to bind, but make sure that you really need it first, otherwise you'll end up with a soggy mix! If you put too much water in it's not really a problem though, just add extra oatmeal.

4. Split the dough into two (makes rolling easier) and roll out on a flour dusted surface until it is about 3 mm (8th of an inch) thick (I like to use spelt flour or fine oatmeal to roll with, but whatever you have will do).

5. Cut with cookie cutter and place onto an oiled oven tray. If you don't have a cookie cutter, then just cut into squares or triangles with a sharp knife.

6. Place on oven tray and then bake in preheated oven between 20 and 25 minutes, until they begin to gently tan.

7. Lift from tray and let them cool down on a cooling tray. They should firm up nicely with an enjoyable crunch. Some people like them less crunchy, in which case take out before they start to tan. I am in the 'crunchy' camp personally. Explore.

Variations and notes:

I make oatmeal (ground oats) from regular organic, rolled oats by grinding them for a few seconds in a nut mill (although you can buy oatmeal ready ground in any decent health food store).

Try making "Really Oaty Oatcakes" instead. If you don't have ground seeds (or a nut mill), then the recipe works well without them. Simply replace the seeds with oatmeal.

Add fresh chopped garden herbs, dried mixed herbs or garlic.

FIVE MINUTE FLAT BREAD

This has got to be the easiest way to create wholesome, scrumptious bread - ever!

Makes: 9 pieces of flat bread
Preparation time: 15 minutes
Cooking time: 5 minutes

Ingredients:

200g of spelt flour
1 tablespoon of tamari
(or sprinkle of sea salt)
Spring water
Rolling pin

Variations:

Try adding a clove of crushed garlic to the mixture.
Add a handful of finely chopped mixed garden herbs.
Add ground seed/nut meal to the flour.
Add a sprinkling of whole, small seeds such as sesame or poppy.

1. Place flour into a mixing bowl and form a well in the centre.

2. Add tamari (or salt) and a little water in the well. Start by 'cutting' the ingredients together with a blunt knife until they begin to bind.

3. Once the mixture begins to bind, use your hands to push mixture together, adding a very little water at a time (IMPORTANT: don't over do it with the water – you are looking to form a dough that is rollable, but not so sticky that it sticks to your hands). Knead until you form a dough (if it does stick to your hands then it is too wet, so try adding a little more spelt flour to balance things out again).

4. Separate the mixture into small balls (a little smaller than golf balls).

5. Roll out each ball evenly onto a lightly floured surface until about 3 mm thick.

6. Place under a medium grill and KEEP YOUR EYE ON THEM because they grill very quickly and if you leave them for a minute too long they will burn. They may begin to rise (like pita bread) depending on the intensity of the heat – a little exciting bonus - and perfectly normal. When they start to get a light tan, turn them over and grill on the other side. You can place a few under the grill at the same time. Grilling will take only a few minutes in total.

MUSHROOM GRAVY

This goes perfectly with the seed loaf on page 104.

Ingredients:
150g mushrooms
1 clove garlic
2 tablespoons olive oil
200ml water
2 heaped teaspoons cornflour
1 heaped teaspoon onion granules
½ teaspoon sea salt

1. Chop mushrooms into very small pieces.

2. Crush garlic.

3. Sauté garlic and mushrooms in the oil for a couple of minutes.

4. Dissolve cornflour into a small amount of water in a jug by mixing rapidly with a spoon. Add the rest of the water to the jug, before pouring into the pan along with the sautéed mushrooms and garlic.

5. Add sea salt and onion granules, keeping the stove on a medium heat.

6. Be sure to stir almost continuously with a wooden spoon, whilst the temperature of the gravy is heating up. The cornflour will quickly thicken the sauce once it reaches boiling point. If you don't keep stirring, then it will probably go lumpy.

7. Cook for another minute or two, whilst stirring, allowing time for the flavours to dance together and then serve.

EASY COCONUT SAUCE

A lovely, simple, no fuss, savoury sauce that works nicely drizzled over plain potatoes or vegetables.

Ingredients:
100g creamed coconut block
300ml spring water
2 heaped teaspoons cornflour
½ pinch sea salt (or tamari to taste)

1. Shave the creamed coconut block with a knife so that it crumbles.

2. Dissolve cornflour into the cold water by whisking rapidly with a spoon.

3. Put everything in the pan together, turning the stove heat to low/medium, whilst stirring.

4. The sauce will thicken as soon as it starts getting hot. Bring to the boil and keep stirring for another minute or two.

Sweet Dessert Alternative:

Make hot sweet coconut sauce for desserts by leaving out the sea salt and replacing with two tablespoons of coconut sugar or rice syrup.

HOMEMADE PASTA SAUCE

I created this recipe for my son as an alternative to the jar bought varieties. The flavours dance wonderfully together if left for a few hours before serving. It works great as a conscious pizza sauce too.

Serves: 3
Preparation: 10 minutes
Cooking: 15 minutes

Ingredients:

Dash of olive oil
Large handful of tasty mushrooms
1 large garlic clove
125ml water
2 heaped teaspoons cornflour
700g of passata (salt free)
1 tablespoon apple juice concentrate
2 tablespoons apple cider vinegar
1 heaped teaspoon ground coriander
1 heaped tablespoon mixed fresh herbs
 (i.e. oregano and parsley) or:
  1 level tablespoon of dried mixed herbs
Pinch of ground chilli (optional)
Sea salt to taste

1. Roughly chop the mushrooms and crush the garlic.

2. Heat a dash of olive oil in a pot or pan and gently sauté the mushrooms and garlic for two to three minutes.

3. In the meantime: Mix the cornflour thoroughly with the cold water. The cornflour needs to be fully mixed in i.e. no lumps or white bits showing.

4. Add the passata, sea salt, apple cider vinegar, apple juice and herbs into the pan along with the cornflour/water mixture.

5. Mix thoroughly whilst heating up and bringing to the boil.

6. Add the ground coriander and chilli powder then allow to simmer for up to ten minutes, stirring frequently.

Other tasty variations:

CORIANDER LEAVES: Add a handful of chopped coriander just before serving.

NO MUSHROOMS: If you don't like mushrooms, then replace with an onion instead.

BASIL: Leave out the ground coriander, chili and mushrooms and add an extra clove of garlic at the start. Add a generous handful of chopped basil, once it has cooked, just before serving (to retain the delicious basil flavour).

OLIVES: Chop pitted olives in half. Add as many as you like to your own preference.

VEGGIE SAUCE: Add chopped courgette and sweet peppers at the sauté stage.

Toasted Seeds

Simple to make.
Surprisingly delicious.

Preparation: 3 minutes
Cooking time: approx 20 minutes baking
(or 7 minutes grilling)

Ingredients:

*A tray of shelled seeds
(i.e. sunflower or pumpkin)*

Tamari or shoyu

1. Place a pile of seeds on a baking tray - about 1cm deep.

2. Sprinkle a dash of tamari or shoyu over the seeds and mix in.

3. Place under a grill (medium heat) and mix in regularly over about 7 minutes **or** place in preheated oven approx gas mark 6 (200°C/400°F) and mix in several times during baking period of about 20 minutes.

4. Pumpkin seeds will pop to indicate that you need to mix them in, otherwise be vigilant and make sure that the seeds don't burn.

Easy snack!

Sweet Treats

I wasn't big into eating desserts, until I started creating conscious kitchen sweet treats. It's very difficult to resist when they taste so delectable! There is undoubtedly something incredibly nurturing about tucking into a delicious homemade sweet treat. The secret is to create them consciously with love and eat in moderation. I often prefer to eat sweet treats as a little snack in the middle of the afternoon, rather than after a meal, although there are no hard and fast rules, other than to enjoy every morsel! In our conscious kitchen the desserts tend to come in full flow when we have guests around for dinner.

CASHEW & VANILLA COOKIES

With a lovely luxurious bite and delicious flavour, cashews make a wonderful addition to this biscuit recipe. I use brown rice syrup to sweeten, coconut oil to bind and a touch of vanilla to make a rich, luxurious treat.

Makes: 8 cookies
Preparation: 10 minutes
Cooking: 12 - 15 minutes

Ingredients:

Dry ingredients:
100g cashew nuts
200g spelt flour

Wet ingredients:
100ml rice syrup
125ml coconut oil
2 teaspoons vanilla extract

1. Turn on oven to gas mark 5 (190°C / 375°F).

2. Crush cashew nuts into small pieces and crumbs by using a pestle and mortar. Alternatively place them into a big bag and crush by rolling over with a rolling pin.

3. Mix all dry ingredients together in a large mixing bowl.

4. Melt coconut oil and then whisk all wet ingredients together.

5. Thoroughly mix wet ingredients into the dry ingredients using a wooden spoon.

6. Make about eight little balls with the mixture, flattening them into cookies about 1cm thick using your hands.

7. Place onto oiled baking tray, leaving about 3cm between each cookie to allow for spreading.

8. Bake for 12 - 15 minutes in your preheated oven. Remove from baking tray with a spatula and then allow to cool on a cooling rack before serving.

CHOCOLATE CHIP COOKIES

Follow the instructions above, replacing the cashews with 50g of vegan chocolate chips and using only 75ml rice syrup instead of 100ml.

Maple Maya Hot Chocolate Drink

Maple maya hot chocolate is like a hug from a best friend on a chilly winters night. It's perfect if you want to whip something up quickly without the bother of getting all the baking tins out.

Serves: 1
Preparation: 5 minutes

Ingredients:

1 mugful of rice milk
1 heaped teaspoon cocoa powder
2 or 3 teaspoons maple syrup
Dash of vanilla extract

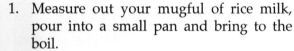

1. Measure out your mugful of rice milk, pour into a small pan and bring to the boil.
2. Meanwhile mix one heaped teaspoon of fair trade cocoa powder in your mug with two teaspoons of maple syrup (adjust the amount to your preferred taste if needed) until it turns into a lovely smooth sauce consistency.
3. When the milk has boiled, quickly pour into the mug and stir.
4. Add a little cold milk if necessary and enjoy!

Variations:

Substitute half of the milk with water for a much lighter drink.
Add a sprinkle of cinnamon to the initial paste.
Use rice syrup instead of maple syrup.
Use hazelnut, almond or hemp milk instead of rice milk.

Apple Flapjacks

In Britain, a flapjack is basically an oat bar that consists of oats, golden syrup and butter. I started with oats and brought in some of my favourite conscious kitchen ingredients to create a recipe that goes down a real treat.

Makes: 8 slices
Preparation: 15 minutes
(plus three hours soaking time)
Cooking time: 20 minutes

Ingredients:

Wet ingredients:
100ml sunflower oil
100ml apple juice concentrate
1 teaspoon almond essence
100g raisins (to be soaked)

Dry ingredients:
300g rolled oats
1 level tablespoon ground cinnamon

Extra things:
Spring water to soak the raisins
A little extra oil to oil baking tray
A baking tray/dish (approx 21cm squared and at least 2cm deep)

1. Soak the raisins well in advance. Three hours will help them to soften nicely. I sometimes soak them overnight if I am preparing food the next morning. When soft, drain off the soak-water.

2. Blend all wet ingredients (this includes the soaked raisins) together in a jug to form a puree. It's fine if you have some raisin chunks in there too, as long as you have a thick sauce-like mixture.

3. Mix oats and cinnamon together in large bowl, creating a well in the middle of the mixture.

4. Pour sauce into the well and mix all ingredients thoroughly together.

5. Press firmly into a well oiled baking tray.

6. Place in a preheated oven on gas mark 6 (200°C/400°F) for approximately 20 minutes.

7. When ready (gently tanned on the top), take them out and score the flapjacks into slices. Leave them in the baking tray to cool down and firm up for a while, before carefully taking them out to serve.

Alternatives:

You can use sultanas/dates/dried apricots instead of raisins.
Use an alternative syrup sweetener, especially if you have a local alternative option.

BANANA & CHOCOLATE CUPCAKES

A deliciously healthy and light cake.

Makes: 8 cupcakes
Preparation: 10 minutes
Cooking: 20 minutes

Ingredients:

Dry ingredients:
1 large ripe banana
150g spelt flour
50g sugar free vegan chocolate
  (or carob)
1 teaspoon bicarbonate of soda

Wet ingredients:
100ml sunflower oil
75ml apple juice concentrate
75ml rice milk
1 teaspoon apple cider vinegar
1 teaspoon vanilla extract

Extra things:

You will need eight large cupcake cases and a deep cupcake tin.

1. Mash banana in mixing bowl.

2. Chop the chocolate into small chips.

3. Add the chocolate chips along with the rest of the dry ingredients to the bowl and mix together.

4. Mix all of the wet ingredients together in a jug, then mix thoroughly with the ingredients in the mixing bowl.

5. Carefully spoon and share out between the cupcake cases in the tin, adding extra cupcake cases if necessary.

6. Bake on the middle shelf of a preheated oven at 200°C (400°F/ gas mark 6) for twenty minutes. The cakes should have risen and the tops should look a little tanned.

7. Take cupcakes out of the tins and leave to cool on a cooling rack before serving.

8. Share with your friends!

Sweet Potato & Ginger Cake

This makes me feel like I am having all the nutritional benefits of dinner for pudding.
It's surprisingly delicious.

Serves: 8 slices
Preparation: 20 minutes
Cooking: 50 minutes (approx)

Ingredients:

Dry ingredients:
150g sweet potato (peeled)
175g spelt flour
75g raisins
1 teaspoon bicarbonate of soda
1 heaped tablespoon desiccated coconut

Wet ingredients:
2 semi-heaped teaspoons grated fresh ginger
Juice of ½ medium sized lemon
100ml sunflower, safflower or coconut oil
75ml brown rice syrup
75ml rice milk
1 teaspoon apple cider vinegar

You'll also need:
A 1lb (450g) loaf tin (approx 22 x 6 x 11 cm)
Parchment paper

1. Turn on your oven to 200°C (gas mark 6 or 400°F) to preheat ahead of time.
2. Line your loaf tin with parchment paper.
3. Peel and grate sweet potato.
4. Add all the dry ingredients into a mixing bowl EXCEPT the desiccated coconut. Mix together.
5. Grate fresh ginger and put in a jug (along with any juice produced by the grating process).
6. Mix all wet ingredients together in jug with the ginger.
7. Mix the dry and wet ingredients together thoroughly with a wooden spoon.
8. Spoon your mixture into the parchment lined loaf tin and then sprinkle desiccated coconut on top.
9. Place in the middle of your preheated oven. Leave for approximately fifty minutes or until a skewer or toothpick comes out without any mixture clinging to it.

Two Minute Tahini Pudding

Tahini pudding is so simple that I almost forgot to include it in this book. You can whip this up in a flash and tuck in a few short moments later. We love tahini pudding!

Option 1:

Banana and Tahini Pudding

Ingredients:

1 heaped tablespoon tahini
Rice milk (2x as much milk as tahini - approx)
1 fully ripe banana

1. Put a dollop of tahini in a bowl.
2. Mix in a little rice milk at a time until you get a creamy texture. Two parts liquid to one part tahini is a good ratio - but play with it.
3. Mash in the banana.
4. Take a deep breath and savour your delicious creation!

Option 2:

Apple and Tahini Pudding

Ingredients:

1 heaped tablespoon tahini
Rice milk (twice as much as tahini - approx)
1 small sweet juicy apple
1 tablespoon desiccated coconut (optional)

1. Put a dollop of tahini in a bowl.
2. Mix in a little rice milk at a time until you get a creamy texture.
3. Finely chop small, sweet, juicy apple and mix in. Sprinkle on desiccated coconut.
4. Depending on the size of the apple, you may need a little more tahini.

Option 3:

Raisin and coconut pudding

Ingredients:

1 heaped tablespoon tahini
Rice milk (twice as much as tahini - approx)
1 tablespoon desiccated coconut
1 heaped tablespoon raisins (or finely chopped dates)

1. Create as above in option 2, replacing apple for raisins and coconut.

ENLIGHTENMENT BY CARROT CAKE

It's hard to imagine that a sweet treat could be so healthful, tasty and nutritious.

Serves: 12 slices
Preparation: 25 minutes (plus soaking)
Cooking: 35 minutes

Ingredients:

Dry ingredients:
300g spelt flour
2 or 3 large carrots (approx 350g)
150g raisins
1 tablespoon bicarbonate of soda
1 tablespoon ground cinnamon
Pinch sea salt

Wet ingredients:
1 heaped teaspoon fresh ginger (grated)
175ml apple juice concentrate ***
150ml coconut oil **
300ml spring water
1 tablespoon apple cider vinegar
1 teaspoon vanilla extract

Frosting ingredients:
150g cashews
150g dates *
1 teaspoon vanilla extract
Spring water to soak

You will also need:
2 round baking tins (20cm diameter)
Parchment paper
Desiccated coconut for decoration

1. Grate carrots.
2. Mix the dry ingredients evenly together in a large mixing bowl.
3. Peel and grate (or finely chop) the ginger (be sure to keep the juice that runs off too).
4. Whisk the wet ingredients thoroughly.
5. Add the wet and dry ingredients together, mixing well.
6. Line two cake tins with parchment paper and share the cake mixture evenly between the two. You can use whatever size tins are available (within reason!) but make sure you adjust cooking time accordingly.
7. Pop into a preheated oven at gas mark 5 (375˚F / 190˚C) and allow to bake for 35 minutes. It is ready when it begins to looked tanned on top and a tooth pick or skewer comes out without any cake sticking to it.
8. Turn it out of the tin onto a cooling rack.

FROSTING:
1. Soak cashews and dates in spring water for a few hours to soften.
2. When soft, discard soak-water then blend cashews, dates and vanilla extract together until creamy.
3. When cake is cool, use ⅓ of frosting to sandwich the two parts together and the remaining amount to coat all over.

Variations:

* Instead of 150g of dates, use 3 tablespoons of rice syrup for the icing.
** Use safflower or sunflower oil if you don't have coconut oil.
*** Try using maple syrup or alternative sweetener instead of apple juice concentrate.

DATE SLICE

This is one of those filling desserts that everyone loves after a hard days work.

Serves: 8 good sized slices
Preparation: 20 minutes (plus soaking)
Cooking: 20 minutes

Ingredients:

Filling ingredients:
300g organic dates

Topping ingredients:
250g rolled oats
75ml brown rice syrup
50ml sunflower oil
50ml coconut oil
1 heaped tablespoon date puree
(from filling)
1 teaspoon vanilla extract

Base ingredients:
150g spelt flour
50ml sunflower oil
2 tablespoons rice syrup

You will also need:

A round, shallow cake tin,
with a pop out bottom,
20cm in diameter or equivalent.

A small splash (approx 5ml) of coconut or
sunflower oil with which to oil the tin.

Base & filling:

1. Soak dates overnight in a jug, completely covering with water. Make sure that the water line is at least 3cm above the dates to allow for swelling.

2. Next day – drain and discard the soak-water from the dates and blend dates with a blender to make a puree.

3. Turn on your oven to gas mark 6 (200°C/400°F).

4. Oil the cake tin evenly all over.

5. Thoroughly mix the base ingredients together, starting with a spoon and then pressing together and binding with your fingers as everything begins to blend.

6. Once the base ingredients are thoroughly combined, pour into the cake tin, firmly and evenly pressing down, until you have a compact, even pastry base layer.

7. Place the date puree on top of the compacted base layer and spread evenly. Save one heaped tablespoon of the date puree mixture for the topping.

Topping:

1. First melt the coconut oil by either standing on a sunny windowsill or in a warm place or by placing your bottle (if glass) in a pan of very hot or boiling water until melted.

2. Thoroughly mix all topping ingredients together in a mixing bowl with a spoon to make a crumble topping. This should be ready when everything has evenly combined together.

3. Place the topping on top of the date puree, spreading evenly, pressing downwards firmly to help it hold together.

4. Place on the top shelf of your preheated oven and bake for approximately 20 minutes until the top is lightly tanned.

5. When baked, mark out slices with a sharp knife. Allow to cool in tin before separating and sharing out.

WILD BERRY CRUMBLE

It fills me with joy to find nature's superfood right on my doorstep and to create a highly nutritious dessert with it! Antioxidant rich blackberries can be found in abundance in hedgerows through Britain from late summer to early autumn. If you don't have access to wild berries, then you can use cultivated ones instead. Raspberries, strawberries, blueberries will work perfectly well. This serves nicely with the 'Sweet Dessert Alternative' Coconut Sauce on page 129.

Serves: 3
Preparation: 15 minutes
Cooking time: 25 minutes

Ingredients:

Topping ingredients:
100g oatmeal
25g sunflower seeds
2 tablespoons coconut oil
2 tablespoons apple juice concentrate
1 teaspoon almond essence

Filling ingredients:
1 small apple
Few handfuls blackberries
1 tablespoon water

1. Mix all topping ingredients together thoroughly with a spoon until you achieve a crumbly consistency.
2. Chop unpeeled apple into small chunks (approximately 1cm cubed) and place in a small pan with a lid on.
3. Put one tablespoon of water in the pan and cook on a medium heat for 2 - 3 minutes. Be sure to stir frequently and place lid back on in between stirring.
4. After taking cooked apple off the heat, mix together with a few handfuls of blackberries and then place in a small oven proof dish. A dish that is 15cm in diameter and 3cm high should work well - but use what you have available.
5. Gently press down the apple and berry filling in the dish and then top with the crumble topping, pressing together so that it begins to hold.
6. Pop into a preheated oven at gas mark 6 (200°C/400°F) and cook for approximately 25 minutes or until the top begins to tan.

TAPIOCA PUDDING

With bountiful, fond childhood memories of our evening meals, I have my lovely mother to thank for my love of creamy milk puddings. Using coconut milk to replace the dairy milk and bringing in dates and maple syrup instead of sugar, I created this super-conscious alternative to tantalise the taste buds.

Serves: 3
Preparation: 5 minutes, plus soaking
Cooking: 15 minutes

Ingredients:

8 pitted dates
75g pearled tapioca
200ml spring water
400ml coconut milk
2 tablespoons maple syrup

1. Chop dates into small pieces and place in the pan with tapioca and water. Allow to soak for about one hour. This is ideal to do whilst preparing your main meal.

2. After about an hour add the coconut milk and bring the pan to the boil. Stir thoroughly to make sure the tapioca doesn't stick to the bottom of the pan.

3. Once it has started to boil and bubble, turn down to a low/medium heat and place a loose lid on the pan. Stir frequently with a wooden spoon, over about ten minutes, or until the tapioca pearls become translucent. The dates should 'melt' in during the cooking period; use your spoon to press them, helping their break down if needed.

4. Stir in maple syrup near the end of the cooking time.

5. By the end of the cooking period, you should have a thick, rich, creamy dessert.

6. Enjoy hot or allow to cool down and have it cold.

Apple & Cinnamon Cakes

Sweet treats really can be so full of goodness that it makes you wonder why anyone would ever want to eat anything else again!

Makes: 12 small cakes
Preparation: 15 minutes
Cooking time: 20 minutes

Ingredients:

Dry ingredients:
150g dessert apples (two small apples)
175g spelt flour
75g raisins
2 tablespoons cinnamon
1 teaspoon bicarbonate of soda

Wet ingredients:
100ml coconut oil
75ml apple juice concentrate
75ml rice milk
1teaspoon apple cider vinegar

You will also need:
A shallow cupcake tin for twelve cakes.
12 cupcake cases.

1. Turn on your oven to gas mark 6 (200°C/400°F).

2. Grate apple.

3. Mix all dried ingredients in a mixing bowl.

4. Melt coconut oil by placing glass bottle in a pan of boiling water for a few minutes or leaving in a warm place/sunny window-sill for a while.

5. Measure all wet ingredients into a jug and stir briefly.

6. Pour wet ingredients into the mixing bowl along with the dry ingredients and mix until everything is mixed in.

7. Place a cupcake case in each cupcake well in the tin and then spoon a good dollop into each case.

8. Bake for about 20 minutes.

No-Bake Carob Cookies

This recipe is a cross between a cookie and a cake offering a rich treat, ideal for special occasions. Carob is a naturally sweet, nutritious little gem. The taste of carob does vary from supplier to supplier. I prefer the lighter varieties, although I do use whatever I can get hold of at the time. If you can find raw carob powder, why not treat yourself!

Serves: 8
Preparation: 15 minutes

Ingredients:

100g oatmeal
120g ground almonds (or sunflower seeds)
70g desiccated coconut
100g carob powder
4 tablespoons date syrup
Spring water to bind
Desiccated coconut to roll with

1. Bind all ingredients together, adding a little water at a time until mixture is just moist enough to bind (to test consistency take a little amount between fingers and see if it sticks together).

2. Take small amounts and roll into balls in the extra coconut on a large plate and then flatten to about 1.5cm in thickness to make small circular cookies.

3. They can be served immediately. Refrigerate any left over. They will keep for days (if you are lucky!) and will grow even more delicious as the flavours mature and dance together.

*"The secret of health for both mind and body
is not to mourn for the past,
not to worry about the future,
or not to anticipate troubles,
but to live the present moment
wisely and earnestly."*

~Siddartha Guatama Buddha~

Raw Chocolate

Making chocolate is such an enjoyable activity in our kitchen that I really wanted to share some of the positive vibes here in my book. Contrary to popular belief, cocoa is said to have many health benefits. Of course the commercial variety is full of refined sugar, dairy and all sorts of things that are best to avoid. However, if you use an organic, fair trade, raw variety along with other wholesome ingredients, it becomes an essential, nutritiously nurturing superfood.

Making your own chocolate basically involves melting the cocoa butter, mixing the ingredients together and pouring them into a mould to chill and set.

You can buy fancy and fun shaped chocolate moulds from your local kitchen monger. Any small, shallow container will do though. I often use little tins or plastic containers with a bit of unbleached parchment paper to line the bottom.

I've listed some suggested recipes on the next page.
Before you get stuck in, here are six easy steps on how to create delicious home-made raw chocolate...

STEP ONE: 'Shave' the solid cocoa butter with a sharp knife or grater. Shaving is just really thin slicing that makes the cocoa butter crumble. The finer you can get it, the easier it will be to melt. You can leave it in big chunks if you like, but be prepared to wait a while for it to melt.

STEP TWO: Melt the cocoa butter. You can do this by leaving it in a warm place in a heat proof glass bowl by a fire or directly above a hot radiator. It melts at 34°C. The idea is to melt it, rather than cook it, maintaining its 'un-cookedness'. If you don't have a gentle heat source then use a hob or stove. Put the cocoa butter in a small, oven proof, glass bowl and then put that bowl in a pan containing an inch or so of really hot water. Keep the hob/stove burning on a low heat. The heat will then transfer through the bowl, enough to melt the cocoa butter. Give it frequent stirs to assist the melting process. Don't keep it on the heat any longer than it takes to melt it. The best time to use it is when it has just melted. If it is too hot, then it takes longer to cool down and the coconut sugar will sink to the bottom of the chocolate when added.

STEP THREE: Add the coconut sugar to the melting cocoa butter during step two. The melting cocoa butter will help to soften and dissolve the sugar.

STEP FOUR: When the cocoa butter has finally melted, mix in the cocoa powder and any other remaining ingredients.

STEP FIVE: Pour your mixture into the mould. If the mixture is too runny, the coconut sugar may sink to the bottom of the container before it sets, in which case, wait a few minutes for the mixture to become a little more viscous before you pour it into the mould.

STEP SIX: Place your chocolate mould into a fridge until it becomes solid (about 20 minutes) or the freezer (if you can't wait). When solid, pop it out of the container and enjoy!

See over page for recipes...

Here are a few ideas to get you started.
Play with them, explore, have fun, design your own favourite.
Think of things that I haven't even listed here.
T = tablespoon   tsp = teaspoon

DARK VANILLA
50g raw cocoa butter
50g raw cocoa powder
3T raw coconut sugar
1 tsp vanilla extract
Sprinkle of cocoa nibs

LUCAMA MELTS
60g raw cocoa butter
4T raw lucama powder
1T raw coconut sugar

FRUIT N' NUT
50g raw cocoa butter
50g raw cocoa powder
3T raw coconut sugar
1T sundried raisins
1T chopped hazelnuts

MANGO MAMMA
40g raw cocoa powder
40g raw cocoa butter
2T raw coconut sugar
15g sundried mango
(finely chopped)

MAGIC MINTS
40g raw cocoa butter
30g raw cocoa powder
30g raw coconut sugar
½ tsp peppermint extract

Raw Chocolate Covered 'Caramels'

These little balls really are manna from heaven - a total superfood, sweet treat feast. Lucama powder (a dried, sweet, fruit packed with nutrients and goodness) plays a key role in this delightful little gem. It adds so much to raw food desserts and is well worth the effort of getting hold of. It's usually available in any good health food store.

Makes: 8 balls
Preparation: 20 minutes
(plus soaking/freezing time)

Ingredients:

100g pitted dates
50g coconut butter
2 tablespoons lucama (25g)
2 tablespoons desiccated coconut
½ portion of 'Dark Vanilla' chocolate
(as on page 152 but without cocoa nibs).

Soak dates overnight in spring water

Next day:

1. Drain dates and blend with coconut butter and lucama. This works best with a hand blender.

2. Put mixture in the fridge or freezer for about 15 minutes to thicken a little before rolling.

3. Once chilled, scoop a heaped teaspoon of the mixture and roll into a small ball. Either roll directly into the desiccated coconut on a plate or directly in your hands without coconut (the oil is great for your hands!).

4. Place the rolled balls onto a tray lined with parchment paper and pop into the freezer for at least half an hour (longer is fine).

5. When you are ready, start to make the dark vanilla chocolate. Keep the chocolate runny (but not too runny) ready for rolling the balls into.

6. Take the caramel balls out of the freezer and dip into the melted chocolate. Place them right back on the parchment paper and when you've covered them all with chocolate, pop them back into the freezer. Freeze for at least 20 minutes before serving. If you aren't ready to serve, just pop them into a container and leave them in the fridge.

"Those who see all creatures in themselves and
themselves in all creatures know no fear.
Those who see all creatures in themselves
and themselves in all creatures know no grief.
How can the multiplicity of life delude
the one who sees its unity?
The Self is everywhere.
Bright is the Self, indivisible, untouched by sin,
wise and transcendent.
She it is who holds the cosmos together."

~Isha Upanishad ~

NOTES FROM MY PANTRY

I've always wanted a pantry - one of those huge, old fashioned walk in cupboards for storing all kind of conscious kitchen goodies. For now, I am happy to enjoy my well loved shelves and cupboards.

It's helpful to have a few things in stock, so that whenever you feel inspired you can magic something up. Here is a little peek into my kitchen and some of the things that I tend to keep in, ready to grab at a moments notice...

THE 'OILS AND BOTTLES' SHELF

Oils - I buy cold pressed, organic oils that have endured as little processing as possible, retaining their vital elements of nutrition. Hemp oil, sunflower oil, olive oil, flax oil, coconut oil and raw cocoa butter are great to have in. I like to use a variety for different essential fats. My firm favourite and ultra high vibrational winner, heads up, is hemp oil. It's jam packed with goodness.

Alternative sweeteners - you can usually find apple juice concentrate, brown rice syrup and date syrup all in my cupboard at any one time. Something for every occasion.

Mustard - ready made type in a jar - ideal for salad dressings. This is handy for a bit of variation. I never used to use this, but everyone else seems to like it, so it eventually found its way into my pantry.

Extracts and essences - good quality vanilla extract and almond essence – an essential little bit of magic, used in small amounts for sweet, baked treats.

Milks and drinks - spring water, rice milk, coconut milk, coconut water. People love to add rice milk and coconut milk to breakfast dishes and smoothies.

Shoyu - is a great sauce to splash on things. It varies enormously in quality. I only buy a good quality, organic shoyu (easily found in health food stores). It is made with fermented soya beans and wheat (although people who are sensitive to wheat or gluten seem to be fine with good quality shoyu in moderation. It is thought that by the end of the brewing process, the gluten has almost all gone).

Tamari - is a wheat-free, stronger tasting variety of shoyu. Shoyu and tamari are inter-changeable in recipes (although they may have ever-so-slightly different strengths).

Apple cider vinegar - makes a regular appearance in the recipes here. It can enliven salad dressings and makes for an unexpected twist in some of the other dishes.

Tahini - is a thick, spreadable, paste made from pure ground sesame seeds. It can be found either raw or roasted. We use it as a thick, creamy base for sauces. We also make puddings with it; spread it on crackers; pop it in smoothies; or when really in need of some serious spiritual grounding, we even eat it off the spoon. Each brand varies in taste and texture quite radically. Raw tahini tastes different to non-raw.

Nuts and seeds 'n' things - A quintessential part of the conscious kitchen, providing essential fats, nutrients and protein. My cupboard always has an assortment of nuts, seeds, dried coconut and olives in it.

Hazelnuts and walnuts - I always live in hope that we can grow and forage enough of these to sustain ourselves with a local harvest.

Sunflower seeds - you can buy these ready shelled by the big-bag-full in any health food shop. Alternatively, grow your own giant sunflowers and shell your own or use them for sunflower green sprouts. When they have been soaked for a few hours, they become an easy to digest, high vibrational food. Soaking unleashes the dormant life-force within them.

Dried fruits - figs, dates, sultanas, raisins. Interesting alternative sweeteners and ideal as a little snack. Best eaten in moderation as not to upset the delicate blood sugar balance (more delicate for some than others).

Dried herbs, spices 'n' things - ground cinnamon, ground coriander, dried parsley, sun-dried tomatoes, sea salt. I prefer fresh foods wherever possible, but to be honest, I find my little stock of dried stuff invaluable and incredibly convenient in a busy world.

Flours & grains - cornflour, spelt flour, oats, wheat-free rice noodles, brown rice, millet, quinoa, rice cakes and corn thins – always organic, of course.

FRESH HERBS

Growing your own, as much as you are able to, is a must in the conscious kitchen. You don't even have to have a garden or a balcony - almost everyone has a windowsill that can be used for fresh herbs. I find basil, coriander, rosemary, thyme, sage, lemon balm and parsley really useful in salads and baking.

FRESH FOODS

We always have an abundance of fresh foods, such as greens, kale, fruits, vegetables in the house, always favouring what's in season locally.

HANDY KITCHEN TOOLS

It's amazing how resourceful and creative we can be when we don't have things we think we need. I have managed with hardly any equipment at all at times and find that there is usually a way around everything. Here are a few things that you might find useful though...

BLENDER - Whatever your budget allows will work fine with this book. I've tried them all over the years, but I almost always end up reaching for the hand blender first. It's small, doesn't take up much space, easy to clean and cuts right down on washing up. Their portability means you can easily clear the blade if it gets clogged. You can exert more downward pressure to blend any awkward ingredients. You just pop a hand blender into a jug and blend. Jug blenders can, however, be more powerful and tend to have a longer life expectancy. If you have one with a nut/seed mill attachment, you'll find it very handy for some of the recipes in this book too.

GRATER - A good quality grater can soon become a good kitchen friend. Ideally you'll have one with different size grating abilities or different ones for different things. It depends on what you are likely to grate. Carrots and cabbage need a regular grater, whilst ginger, lemon rind and nutmeg require a finer grate.

KNIVES - Every budding kitchen chef has their favourite knife. In fact, if you invest in one thing only, let it be a good quality knife. It can turn slicing and chopping into a joyful work of art. You don't necessarily need a whole selection - I tend to use the same two knives for just about everything.

BAKEWARE & COOKWARE - Personally, I avoid aluminium cookware and non-stick products (i.e. teflon) because they are known to leach toxins. Aside from that, bakeware and cookware is a personal preference. Do some research on the web for healthy and environmentally friendly products. Information is changing all the time. See what feels right for you.

> What to use:
> **GLASS:** For higher vibrational baking, I recommend oven proof, glass products. They can be found in the form of baking trays, pans and even loaf 'tins'. A word of caution though - you must let it cool down a little before putting it on a cold surface or in the kitchen sink. Sudden changes in temperature may cause it to shatter. When serving, always place on a wooden board or thick towel. If you take care, then glass can be an absolute joy to work with. I love it.
> **STAINLESS STEEL & CAST IRON:** Stainless steel is also said to be stable and has been proven to be less prone to leaching than other metal cookware, making it a more desirable choice to use. Cast iron cookware is quite favoured by many conscious cooks, as any leaching of iron is considered a valuable addition to the diet. I have never used it personally, so I can't comment from experience.

WEIGHING SCALES - In true European style this book uses metric measurements to define required quantities. You can work without them if you prefer to use cups to scoop instead, as long as you are happy to do the conversions (see *pages 160 - 162* for conversion charts). Using metric to measure is however, going to keep you closest to the original recipes. I initially designed most of my recipes by using a random mug to measure everything. Actually, it was always more of a 'lovingly throwing in a bit of this and that'. You don't need to measure anything when you are creating. In the spirit of creating a formula for things, I eventually relented and decided for purposes of sharing recipes, to quantify everything more accurately. So, I have befriended metric measurements as an awesome way to share the delicious recipes in this book.

SPOONS - I love spoons for measuring things. Throughout this book I use the following spoons as follows:

Teaspoon = 5ml
Dessertspoon = 10ml
Tablespoon = 15ml

I recommend buying a set of measuring spoons from a kitchen shop if you are unsure about the size of the spoons in your kitchen drawer.

THE JOYS OF INTERNATIONAL MEASURING

There are different ways to measure things all over the world. This book was designed with metric measurements in mind, so I'd highly recommend using metric scales to yield the best results. However, as international as we all are, that is not always possible, in which case, I've drawn up several conversion charts to try and make life a little easier. I am focussing primarily on the US, Australian and British/European systems to simplify things. This can be a bit of a brain scramble, so please bear with me and hold on to your hats!

GRAMMES, CUPS OR OUNCES?

Cups offer a handy way of scooping your ingredients and work best if someone created a recipe with cups right from the start. They are however, not conversion friendly.

Australian and Canadian cups measure 250ml. US cups measure 240ml.

Liquid measurements are easier to convert (see page opposite for chart). By nature, dry foods become complex because they depend on the density of the food you are measuring (unlike liquids which are measured by volume, not weight). For example, 1 cup of desiccated coconut is going to weigh a lot less than one cup of sunflower seeds. There doesn't seem to be a standard conversion for dry stuff that everyone completely agrees on, so I took the liberty of measuring some of the main ingredients in this book myself and coming up with conversions for 1 cup and a ½ cup measurements (somewhere between a US and Canadian cup). I concluded that converting from metric is much easier if you have weighing scales that display ounces and pounds on it. Conversions to imperial are much easier than to cups and are more likely to yield satisfying results. Better still (and recommended), if you have scales that measure in metric, you won't need to convert a thing!

Metric	Non-Metric
A general conversion chart for everything that may be relevant in this book.	
1cm	0.39in
100g	3.53oz
1kg	2lb 3oz
100ml	3.381 US fl oz
0°C	32°F
240ml	1 cup (US)
250ml	1 cup (Canada/Australia)
5ml	1 teaspoon
15ml	1 tablespoon

It's fairly easy if you are converting liquid measurements
because they have standard conversions as follows below:

An Australian or Canadian cup is 250ml.
A US cup is 240ml.

Ideally you'll have a measuring jug that lists ml or fluid oz for
a more accurate conversion.

Liquid measurements			
Metric	US Imperial	Canadian/Australian cups	US Cups
25ml	1fl oz		
60ml	2fl oz	¼ cup	¼ cup
75ml	2½fl oz	⅓ cup	⅓ cup
100ml	3½fl oz		
125ml	4¼ fl oz	½ cup	½ cup
150ml	5fl oz	⅔cup	⅔cup
175ml	6fl oz	¾ cup	¾ cup
200ml	6¾fl oz		
250ml	8½fl oz	1 cup	1 cup
300ml	10fl oz/½ pint	1 ⅓ cup	1¼ cups
350ml	12fl oz	1 ½ cups	1 ½ cups
400ml	13½fl oz	1 ¾ cups	1 ¾ cups
450ml	15fl oz	2 cups	2 cups
473ml	16fl oz (1 US pt)	2 cups	2 cups
500ml	17fl oz		
750ml	25fl oz	3⅓ cups	
1 litre	40fl oz	4⅓ cups	4¼ cups

Note: these charts involve a little rounding up to the nearest whole and sensible figure. A tiny little extra or little less, really shouldn't make much difference.

For dried weight conversions please see over page...

You can get a fairly accurate conversion by using imperial weighing scales to convert as follows

Grammes to ounces	
Metric	**US Imperial**
15g	½ oz
20g	¾ oz
30g	1 oz
40g	1½oz
50g	1¾oz
60g	2oz
75g	2½oz
100g	3½oz
125g	4oz
140g	4½oz
150g	5 ⅓oz
175g	6oz
200g	7oz
225g	8oz
250g	9oz
275g	10oz
300g	11oz
350g	12oz
375g	13oz
400g	14oz
425g	15oz
450g	16oz (1lb)
500g	18oz
750g	1lb 11oz
1kg	2¼lb

Converting from grammes to cups can be a bit more iffy. Some recipes really don't mind a bit of variation. Creating recipes offers the perfect opportunity to embrace your intuition and feel what's right.

Ingredients in grammes to cups		
Ingredient	**1 cup**	**½ cup**
Raisins	200g	100g
Rolled oats	90g	45g
Oatmeal	100g	50g
Spelt flour	120/130g	60/65g
Nuts	150g	75g
Nuts/seeds (ground)	120g	60g
Syrup	310/340g	170g
Chocolate chips	150g	75g
Cocoa powder	85/130g	65g
Desiccated coconut	70g	35g

CONSCIOUS LIVING RESOURCES

Here, I've listed a few of my favourite ethical and conscious living resources.

CONSCIOUS FOOD

Happy Cow is an excellent, free international resource assisting travellers and people everywhere to find vegan, vegetarian and healthy food restaurants, cafes and services. My first port of call online whenever I am travelling.
www.happycow.net

The Vegan Society is the world's original Vegan Society and the actual creator of the word vegan. Established in 1944, it is a trustworthy resource that promotes ways of living free from animal products for the benefit of sentient life.
www.vegansociety.com

Earthfare is an awesome health food store based in Glastonbury UK. You can purchase almost everything listed in this book from their online store.
www.earthfare.co.uk

SPIRITUAL LIFE

Openhand Foundation is a not for profit organisation dedicated to catalysing the evolution and ascension of humankind through unravelling blockages, karma and embracing the truth of our whole, complete beingness. Openhand is the birth place of Trinity's Conscious Kitchen. It offers free meditations, videos and a huge archive of spiritual articles for all to benefit from.
www.Openhandweb.org

ETHICAL LIVING

Traidcraft run development programs in some of the poorest countries in the world and campaign in the UK and internationally to bring about trade justice. They have a lovely on-line shop.
www.traidcraft.co.uk

Ethical Consumer is a magazine and online guide, offering product info for just about anything from appliances to banking and transport.
www.ethicalconsumer.org

ALTERNATIVE LIFESTYLE

Once our inner vibration starts to rise, we often start looking for ways to unravel the system that held us back for so long. There are so many great resources out there once you start looking. Feel the pull to wherever your heart takes you. Here are a few ideas to get you started...

Transition Towns Network is a charitable organisation dedicated to supporting and training communities to acheive self reliance.
www.transitionnetwork.org

WWOOF organisations connect people who want to live and learn on organic farms or smallholdings with people who are looking for volunteers.
www.wwoofinternational.org

LETS (local exchange trading scheme) is an international organisation that facilitates the exchange of goods and skills using LETS credits instead of traditional money. Here's the UK website, but do a web search for your local group.
www.letslinkuk.net

HelpX is an online listing of host farms, homes, lodges, B&Bs, backpackers hostels etc who invite volunteer helpers to stay with them short-term in exchange for food and accommodation.
www.helpx.net

Permaculture Research Institute is a global network committed to sustainable solutions using permaculture methods.
www.permaculturenews.org

Real seeds
A small, UK based local company selling heirloom and heritage seeds. They actually encourage their customers to save their own seed, providing handy seed saving instructions with every order.
www.realseeds.co.uk

Recipe Index